CW01496387

COGNITIVE BEHAVIORAL THERAPY FOR ANXIETY AND DEPRESSION

PRACTICAL TECHNIQUES TO OVERCOME NEGATIVE
THOUGHTS, BUILD A HAPPIER LIFE AND TRANSFORM
YOUR MINDSET FOR LASTING WELL-BEING AND
IMPROVED MENTAL HEALTH

DOTTY LYNN

CONTENTS

INTRODUCTION

Years ago, I sat in a quiet room, feeling the weight of my thoughts pressing down on me. Anxiety and doubt had become constant companions, whispering in my ear that I was not enough. During this time, I stumbled upon Cognitive Behavioral Therapy (CBT). Seeing my struggle, a friend handed me a book on the subject. As I flipped through the pages, I recognized that I was gaining a new perspective on understanding my thoughts and emotions. It was like a door had opened, revealing a path to a place of hope and clarity I had never imagined. This first encounter with CBT transformed my perspective on mental health. It ignited my passion for helping others find their paths to healing.

In today's fast-paced world, anxiety and depression have become all too common. Studies indicate that millions of people worldwide experience these challenges daily. CBT has emerged as a crucial tool in managing these conditions. It offers practical strategies to change negative thought patterns and behaviors. Research supports its effectiveness, making it a widely accepted treatment method.

This book serves as a practical guide for those who want to understand and manage their anxiety and depression. It provides actionable strategies and exercises you can apply daily to foster long-term well-being. Through this guide, I hope to empower you to take control of your mental health journey.

What sets this book apart is its unique approach. It combines psychological research with relatable examples and case studies, allowing for a more in-depth understanding of anxiety and depression. Instead of viewing these conditions as weaknesses, this book encourages you to see them as challenges you can manage. Through empowerment and resilience, change is possible.

As you read through this book, you will gain a better understanding of CBT techniques. You will build emotional resilience and discover practical tools to improve your quality of life. These benefits are not just theories. They are achievable outcomes that significantly enhance your mental health and daily functioning.

Please view this book as a starting point for ongoing learning and growth. Engage with the material actively. Apply the exercises and embrace this journey toward improved mental health. This is more than just a book to read. It is a guide to live by.

The book's structure provides a clear roadmap. It begins by exploring the foundations of CBT and its principles. Then, it delves into specific techniques for managing anxiety and depression. Each chapter builds on the last, providing a comprehensive toolkit for change. You will find themes and sections that make the content easy to navigate and apply.

As you embark on this journey, it is essential to set realistic expectations. Understanding and managing anxiety and depression is an ongoing process. It requires patience and commitment. But with practical strategies and dedication, lasting change is within reach. This book is here to support you every step of the way.

Through this guide, I hope to shift the narrative around anxiety and depression. From one of weakness and shame to empowerment and resilience. Together, we can transform how we view and manage these challenges. Let this book be your companion on the path to improved mental health and a happier, more fulfilling life.

Terms and Definition:

1. **CBT** - Cognitive behavioral therapy: Used to treat anxiety and depression, a type of psychotherapy that helps people manage mental health issues by changing their negative thought patterns and behaviors.
2. **Mindfulness** - A technique that enhances awareness of the present moment, allowing individuals to observe their thoughts, feelings, and bodily sensations without judgment.
3. **Anxiety** - Intense, excessive, and persistent worry and fear about everyday situations. Fast heart rate, rapid breathing, sweating, and tiredness may occur.

4. **Depression** - A mental health condition that can cause severe functional impairment and lower quality of life. Symptoms include feelings of sadness, hopelessness, and loss of interest and activities.

5. **SMART Goals** - Specific, Measurable, Achievable, Relevant, and Time-Bound.

6. **Cognitive Reframing** - This psychological technique helps people change their thoughts about events, situations, and emotions.

7. **Cognitive Restructuring** - A therapeutic technique that helps people identify and replace negative thought patterns with more positive ones.

8. **Exposure Therapy** - Helps people cope with their fears instead of avoiding them.

9. **Social Anxiety** - A chronic mental health condition in which social interactions cause irrational anxiety.

10. **Body Scan** - A mindfulness meditation practice that focuses on the body's physical sensations, such as tension, pain, or discomfort, without judgment.

11. **Mindfulness reflection** - Encourages reflection on thoughts and feelings with curiosity.

12. **Digital tools:**
    - **Daylio** - Helps users track their moods without writing down their feelings.
    - **Moodpath** - A self-management app for mental health disorders like depression, anxiety, and eating disorders. It uses a questionnaire to ask users about their mood and life and then generates a report on their Mental Health.

1

UNDERSTANDING THE FOUNDATIONS OF CBT

S itting across from my first therapist, I remember the room's quiet hum and the gentle ticking of a clock. Someone introduced me to something called Cognitive Behavioral Therapy, or CBT. My therapist spoke about how our thoughts, emotions, and behaviors intertwine, shaping our mental landscape. At the time, I was skeptical, feeling caught in my storm of anxiety and depression. However, as we began exploring CBT, a sense of clarity emerged. It was as if the fog lifted, revealing a path I hadn't seen before. This was a transformative moment, as I not only gained a deeper understanding of my mental health but also realized that change was possible. This chapter is an invitation to discover how CBT can be a guiding light in navigating the complexities of anxiety and depression.

1.1 THE BASICS OF COGNITIVE BEHAVIORAL THERAPY

Cognitive Behavioral Therapy is not just a method; it's a structured approach to psychotherapy that targets specific issues by focusing on the intricate relationship between thoughts, emotions, and behaviors. This approach, developed by Aaron T. Beck in the 1960s, revolutionized how we understand mental health. Beck's work suggested that it's not just the situations we face that affect us but our interpretations of these situations that genuinely matter. This insight laid the foundation for CBT, which has since grown into a globally influential therapy, proven effective in over 2000 clinical trials for various mental disorders (SOURCE 1).

CBT sessions are typically structured to provide a clear framework for addressing your concerns. These sessions often involve setting specific goals and completing practical homework assignments. This structured approach helps you gradually apply the insights gained during therapy to real-world situations. Typically, CBT is time-limited, with most therapy courses lasting between 6 and 20 sessions. This format enables a focused and intensive exploration of your issues. This format allows you to see progress within a relatively short period, encouraging continued engagement and effort.

The core principles of CBT are grounded in the cognitive model, which is centered on understanding and changing negative thought patterns. By identifying these patterns, you can alter the behaviors and emotions that stem from them. Behavioral interventions, such as exposure therapy, are also integral to CBT. These interventions help you confront and manage the fears and situations that contribute to your anxiety or depression. This collaborative effort between you and your therapist fosters a sense of partnership, where you work together as co-investigators in understanding and overcoming your mental health challenges.

Its focus on the present makes CBT distinct from other therapeutic approaches. Unlike psychoanalysis, which often delves into experiences to uncover unconscious conflicts, CBT emphasizes the here and now, working to change current thought patterns and behaviors (SOURCE 2). While medication can be a valuable tool in managing symptoms, CBT offers a way to address the underlying cognitive processes, providing a more sustainable and empowering approach to mental health.

One of CBT's greatest strengths is its adaptability. Whether through traditional face-to-face sessions, online therapy platforms, or self-help workbooks and apps, you can tailor CBT to fit your lifestyle and preferences. Digital resources make CBT more accessible than ever, allowing you to engage with therapy at your own pace and convenience. This flexibility ensures that CBT can be a viable option for many, regardless of their circumstances.

Reflection Section

Think about a recent situation where your thoughts might have influenced your emotions or actions. Consider how you interpreted the problem and what thoughts arose. Write down these thoughts and reflect on how they impacted your feelings and behaviors. This exercise is the first step in recognizing patterns and beginning to change them.

As we continue to explore the foundations of CBT, remember that understanding these concepts is not just an academic exercise. It's a practical step towards reclaiming control over your thoughts and emotions, paving the way for a more balanced and fulfilling life.

1.2 HOW THOUGHTS INFLUENCE EMOTIONS AND BEHAVIORS

Imagine waking up on a Monday morning, overwhelmed by the week ahead. The simple idea of facing a project you've been putting off fills you with dread. It is a classic example of the thought-emotion-behavior cycle that CBT aims to address. The cycle begins with a thought—"I'll never finish this project"—which gives rise to an emotional response, such as anxiety or fear. This emotional state then influences behavior, often leading to procrastination. As the deadline looms, the anxiety intensifies, creating a negative spiral. In this cycle, our thoughts are the starting point, setting off a chain reaction that affects how we feel and act. Understanding this relationship is crucial because it highlights our power to change our emotional and behavioral outcomes by modifying our thoughts.

At the heart of this cycle are automatic thoughts. These spontaneous, often unconscious reactions pop into our minds without deliberate effort. They can be damaging and self-critical, such as "I'm a failure" or "I can't handle this." These thoughts are not harmless; they contribute significantly to emotional distress and can lead to behaviors that reinforce negative beliefs. For instance, believing you are a failure might lead you to avoid challenging tasks and confirm your doubts. Cognitive restructuring, a central technique in CBT, involves identifying and challenging these automatic thoughts. You can alter your emotional responses and behaviors by questioning their validity and replacing them with more balanced, rational thoughts.

To illustrate the power of changing thoughts, consider a case where someone struggles with social anxiety. They might think, "Everyone will judge me if I speak up." This thought can lead to avoidance, reinforcing their fear of judgment. By using CBT techniques like Socratic questioning, they can challenge this belief. Questions such as, "What evidence do I have that supports this thought?" or "What would a friend say about this situation?" can help reframe the thought into something like, "Some people might not agree with me, but that's okay." This shift can reduce anxiety and encourage more positive social interactions. Such thought modification demonstrates the profound impact of cognitive restructuring on emotional states.

Cognitive distortions add another layer to this understanding. These exaggerated or irrational thought patterns can skew our perception of reality. A typical distortion is all-or-nothing thinking, where situations are seen in black-and-white terms without any middle ground. For example, you might think, "If I don't do this perfectly, I've failed." Recognizing these distortions is the first step in addressing them. Exercises such as journaling can help identify distorted thinking patterns, allowing you to gradually replace them with more realistic and flexible thoughts. In doing so, you open yourself to a broader range of emotional and behavioral responses, reducing the likelihood of falling into negative spirals.

Exercise: Identifying Cognitive Distortions - *"Let's grab a pen and paper! It'll be great to take some notes to help keep everything organized as we go."*

Take a moment to reflect on a recent situation where you experienced strong emotions. Write down the thoughts you had at the time. Look for any patterns or distortions, such as all-or-nothing thinking. Challenge these thoughts by considering alternative interpretations. Write down these new thoughts and reflect on how they might change your emotional response.

By engaging with these exercises and concepts, you empower yourself to break free from the automatic patterns that contribute to anxiety and depression. This process is not about denying or suppressing negative thoughts but rather about transforming them into opportunities for growth and change. As you continue to explore these ideas, remember that the goal is to create a more balanced and fulfilling mental landscape.

1.3 IDENTIFYING COMMON COGNITIVE DISTORTIONS

Cognitive distortions are sneaky, irrational thoughts that can twist our perception of reality, often without us even realizing it. They are like funhouse mirrors, warping the truth and skewing how we see ourselves and the world around us. In the context of Cognitive Behavioral Therapy, understanding these distortions is crucial, as they contribute significantly to anxiety and depression by feeding into negative thought cycles. When we fall prey to these distorted patterns, we might feel trapped in a maze of self-doubt and hopelessness. Recognizing and challenging these distortions can help us dismantle the walls they build around us, opening up new possibilities for healthier thinking and emotional resilience.

Overgeneralization is one of the most common cognitive distortions. It involves drawing broad conclusions from a single event or a small piece of evidence. Imagine you receive constructive criticism at work and suddenly think, "I always mess up," or "I'll never get it right." This way of thinking ignores all the times you've succeeded and learned from your experiences. It's like looking at a tiny puzzle piece and assuming you know the whole picture. Catastrophizing takes this further, where you expect the worst-case scenario in every situation. You might be waiting for a friend who is late and instantly worry that something terrible has happened. This distortion amplifies anxiety, making you feel like you're standing on the edge of a cliff, fearing a fall that may never happen.

Another common distortion is personalization, where you take things personally and attribute external events to yourself. Suppose a colleague seems distant one day, and you immediately think it's because of something you did. This mindset can make you feel like you're constantly under a microscope, leading to unnecessary guilt and confusion. Then there's mind reading, assuming you know what others are thinking without concrete evidence. That inner voice tells you, "They must think I'm boring," during a conversation, even though there are no signs of disinterest. These distortions create barriers to authentic communication and self-expression, as they fill the gaps with assumptions rather than facts.

To tackle these distortions, we must shine a light on them through deliberate reflection. Journaling can be an effective tool for this. By writing down your thoughts and analyzing them, you can see patterns in how you think and react. Thought records serve as another structured way to document and dissect your thoughts. They help you track situations, reactions, and potential distortions, allowing you to challenge these thoughts with evidence and alternative perspectives. This practice empowers you to take a step back and objectively evaluate your thoughts, leading to a gradual shift towards healthier thinking patterns.

Guided Exercise: Identifying Cognitive Distortions

Think of a recent situation that triggered a strong emotional response. Write down the event details, your initial thoughts, and your feelings. Review your thoughts and identify distortions, such as overgeneralization or mind reading. Ask yourself, "What evidence supports this thought?" and "Is there another way to view this situation?" Document alternative, more balanced thoughts, and reflect on how these new perspectives might change your feelings and reactions.

Consider a scenario where you face workplace stress. Your manager offers some feedback, and you start thinking, "I'm terrible at my job," a classic case of overgeneralization. By recognizing this distortion, you can challenge it with facts: you've received positive reviews in the past and completed several successful projects. This exercise helps break the cycle of distorted thinking, allowing you to approach similar situations with a more evident, grounded mindset. Regularly practicing these techniques strengthens the mental muscles needed to counteract cognitive distortions, paving the way for a more balanced and resilient outlook on life.

1.4 THE SCIENCE BEHIND CBT: EVIDENCE AND EFFICACY

Cognitive Behavioral Therapy (CBT) stands as a beacon of hope in the world of mental health, offering well-documented efficacy through rigorous scientific study. The foundation of CBT's credibility lies in numerous meta-analyses consistently highlighting its remarkable success rates. These studies aggregate findings from multiple trials, providing a comprehensive overview of CBT's impact across various populations. For instance, one meta-analysis revealed that CBT outperforms placebo treatments and is often comparable, if not superior, to medication in managing anxiety and depression. Such data underscores the robustness of CBT as a therapeutic approach, reinforcing its status as a frontline treatment for these prevalent mental health issues.

Beyond short-term success, longitudinal studies offer compelling evidence of CBT's enduring benefits. These studies track individuals over extended periods, revealing that those who undergo CBT experience lasting changes in their mental health. The therapies focus on equipping individuals with the skills to effectively manage their thoughts and emotions, contributing to this durability. Unlike temporary relief treatments, CBT fosters lasting change by promoting self-awareness and cognitive skills that endure well beyond the therapy's conclusion. This capacity for sustained improvement is a testament to CBT's unique approach, which empowers individuals to become their therapists in many respects.

Delving deeper, CBT's mechanisms of change are fascinating and complex. At a neurobiological level, engaging in CBT can significantly change brain activity. Neuroimaging research has shown that CBT can alter neural pathways, particularly those involved in emotion regulation and cognitive processing. This neuroplasticity—the brain's ability to reorganize itself by forming new neural connections—illustrates how

CBT can fundamentally reshape how individuals process and respond to stressors. Additionally, the behavioral changes encouraged by CBT, such as confronting fears or altering habitual responses, further reinforce these neural adaptations, creating a positive feedback loop of cognitive and emotional transformation.

CBT consistently stands out due to its practical and evidence-based framework compared to other therapeutic approaches. For instance, studies comparing CBT to medication for depression often find CBT to be equally effective, with the added benefit of equipping individuals with enduring coping strategies. Unlike medications, which can carry side effects and sometimes result in dependency, CBT empowers individuals to actively engage in their recovery process. Moreover, comparative studies with alternative therapies, such as psychoanalysis, highlight CBT's efficiency and structured nature. While psychoanalysis may delve into the depths of one's experiences, CBT focuses on actionable change in the present, making it a preferred choice for those seeking tangible results in a shorter time frame.

Despite its proven efficacy, CBT has some misconceptions. Some view it as a "quick fix," expecting immediate results without recognizing the effort required to change long-standing thought patterns. This misconception overlooks the depth and commitment involved in CBT, which, while time-limited, demands active participation and practice. Furthermore, skeptics may question CBT's applicability, doubting whether such a structured approach can address the complexities of individual experiences. However, the adaptability of CBT, with its tailored techniques and flexibility in addressing diverse mental health issues, demonstrates its depth and scope. CBT's strength lies in its ability to meet individuals where they are, guiding them through a process of change that is both deeply personal and universally applicable.

1.5 OVERCOMING INITIAL SKEPTICISM: WHY CBT WORKS

When first hearing about Cognitive Behavioral Therapy, many people doubt its structured nature. They might worry that it feels too formulaic or rigid as if it doesn't allow for the nuances of individual experiences. This skepticism is understandable, especially when we are accustomed to thinking of therapy as a profoundly personal and fluid process. However, the structure of CBT is not meant to confine; instead, it provides a clear pathway through which one can navigate the complexities of one's mind. Each session builds upon the last, offering a sense of continuity and progress that can be incredibly grounding for those overwhelmed by their thoughts and emotions.

Another common concern is the effectiveness of self-guided CBT methods. It may seem intimidating in a world that considers professional guidance as essential. Yet, self-guided CBT offers a level of flexibility and accessibility that can be empowering. It allows you to explore techniques at your own pace, fitting them into your life in a way that makes sense. Many find that this autonomy enhances their commitment to the process, which requires active participation and personal responsibility. It's like learning to ride a bike; initially, you might need support, but you gain confidence and independence with practice.

The true impact of CBT becomes evident when we look at personal stories of transformation. For instance, consider a young adult who struggles with social anxiety, feeling paralyzed at the thought of speaking in public. Through CBT, they learned to reframe their fears, gradually exposing themselves to anxiety-inducing situations in a controlled and supportive manner. Over time, they experienced a profound shift, realizing that their anxiety no longer held the same power over them. This transformation didn't happen overnight, but they found a new sense of freedom and self-assurance through steady, intentional work.

Similarly, individuals managing depression have found solace in CBT techniques. They have lifted themselves from despair by actively challenging negative thought patterns and engaging in behavioral activation. Personal accounts highlight how these individuals could reclaim their days, find joy in activities they once enjoyed, and build a meaningful life. These narratives remind us that change is possible, even when it feels unreachable.

One of CBT's greatest strengths is its adaptability to individual needs. It can be customized to address a variety of anxiety disorders, ensuring that the techniques resonate with each person's unique experiences. Whether you're dealing with generalized anxiety, panic disorder, or specific phobias, CBT offers a toolkit that you can customize to fit your challenges. This adaptability also extends across age groups, making CBT a viable option for young people navigating adolescence and adults facing the stresses of later life. Its principles remain consistent, but the application can vary to suit the context of each person's life.

The long-term benefits of CBT are significant, especially compared to some treatments that only provide temporary relief. CBT fosters lasting change by equipping individuals with lifelong coping strategies. These tools encourage self-efficacy, empowering you to manage your mental health proactively. As you practice these techniques, you build a reservoir of resilience that can support you through life's inevitable ups and downs. It's a gradual process that leads to a more stable and fulfilling existence.

In embracing CBT, you open the door to a world of possibilities. It offers a way to cope and a path to thrive. By engaging with its methods, you take the first step toward a life defined not by your struggles but by your strengths. This journey is not just about surviving; it's about flourishing as you navigate your mental landscape with confidence and clarity.

With CBT as your guide, you embark on a journey of self-discovery and empowerment that promises lasting well-being and improved mental health.

2

OVERCOMING NEGATIVE
THOUGHT PATTERNS

I magine waking up each morning to a voice that whispers doubt into your ear, questioning your every move and potential for success. This voice might tell you, "I'm not good enough," or "I'll never succeed." Such phrases are not merely fleeting thoughts; they are the manifestations of negative self-talk many of us experience daily. Negative self-talk can be insidious, weaving its way into our consciousness and reinforcing feelings of inadequacy and low self-esteem. It's like a constant shadow, casting doubt on even the sunniest days. The more we listen to this internal critic, the more we believe its harsh words, allowing it to shape our views and limit our potential. This pervasive negativity can contribute to anxiety and depression, creating a cycle that feels difficult to break.

Understanding the difference between constructive and destructive self-talk is crucial. Constructive self-talk acts as a motivator, encouraging problem-solving and resilience. It sounds like a supportive friend, saying, "You can handle this," or, "Let's find a solution." On the other hand, destructive self-talk is the harsh criticism that feeds self-doubt and blame, whispering, "You always mess up," or, "Why even try?" This harmful dialogue can lead to a downward spiral of negative emotions and behaviors. Recognizing these patterns is the first step in dismantling their power over us. By becoming more aware of the language we use with ourselves, we can begin to shift away from self-blame towards self-compassion.

Self-awareness plays a pivotal role in identifying negative self-talk. Mindfulness practices can be particularly effective in helping us stay present with our thoughts, allowing us to observe them without judgment. By pausing and noticing our internal dialogue, we can see patterns and triggers that may have gone unnoticed. Journaling also offers a powerful method for recording daily thoughts and reflecting on their impact. When we put pen to paper, we create a tangible record of our inner world, making it easier to spot recurring themes. Over time, this practice can reveal insights into how our thoughts influence our emotions and actions, providing a foundation for change.

To alter self-talk patterns, we need tools and techniques to integrate into our daily lives. One effective method is to keep a daily reflection log, noting instances of negative self-talk and the situations that trigger them. This exercise encourages accountability and can help us track progress over time. Another helpful technique is the use of positive affirmations. These empowering phrases replace negative thoughts, such as "I am capable" or "I am worthy of love and respect." We can gradually rewire our brains to adopt a more positive and supportive narrative by consciously repeating these affirmations

Exercise: Tracking and Replacing Negative Self-Talk

Each day, take a few moments to jot down any negative self-talk you notice. Write the situation, the exact words, and how they made you feel. Then, create a positive affirmation to counter each negative phrase. For example, replace "I'm not good enough" with "I am learning and growing each day." Practice saying these affirmations aloud, letting their positivity resonate and diminish the negative voice.

The journey to overcoming negative thought patterns is ongoing and requires patience and persistence. We can transform our internal dialogue by cultivating self-awareness and employing techniques like journaling and positive affirmations. This transformation enhances our mental health and empowers us to live more authentically and confidently. Each slight shift in self-talk is a step towards a more compassionate and fulfilling life.

2.1 TECHNIQUES FOR REFRAMING NEGATIVE THOUGHTS

Imagine seeing the world through a lens that distorts reality, making everything appear darker and more daunting than it truly is. This is where cognitive reframing becomes relevant. It's a powerful tool that allows you to change how you perceive situations. Cognitive reframing is about altering the "frame" through which you view challenging circumstances or distressing thoughts. By shifting your perspective, you can transform a seemingly negative situation into a manageable and even enlightening one. This technique is not about denying reality but recognizing multiple interpretations and choosing the one that serves you best. One effective strategy for reframing involves perspective-taking. It means deliberately trying to see a situation from a different viewpoint. It's akin to stepping into someone else's shoes and understanding how they might perceive the situation.

Example of Cognitive Reframing:

Let's say, after making a mistake at work, you find yourself thinking, "I always mess things up."

1. **Identify the Negative Thought:** Recognize the thought when it arises. In this case, it's the belief that you "always" make mistakes.
2. **Challenge the Thought:** Ask yourself questions to challenge its validity, such as:
   ○ Is it true that I always mess things up?
   ○ Are there times when I've done well or succeeded?
   ○ What evidence do I have that contradicts this thought?
3. **Reframe The Thought:** Replace the negative thought with a more balanced perspective. For example:
   ○ "I made a mistake this time, but I've learned from it and can improve next time."
   ○ "Everyone makes mistakes; they're a part of learning."
4. **Focus on Action:** Shift your attention to what you can do moving forward. You may ask a colleague for

feedback or take some time to review your work process.

5. **Practice Self-Compassion:** Remind yourself that making mistakes is human and doesn't Define your overall abilities or worth.

By using cognitive reframing in this way, you not only interrupt the cycle of negativity but also create a more positive and realistic mindset that encourages growth and resilience. This strategy can be applied to various situations, helping you see challenges as learning opportunities rather than confirming negative beliefs about yourself.

This process can illuminate aspects you hadn't considered and help dispel the negativity clouding your judgment. Another method is questioning assumptions, which involves challenging the validity of the negative thoughts that arise. Ask yourself: "Is this thought based on fact, or is it simply my interpretation?" Often, we find that our thoughts are assumptions rather than truths, and by questioning them, we can open the door to more balanced perspectives.

The benefits of positive reinterpretation extend beyond just a change in thinking. Reframing can lead to healthier emotional responses, lifting the weight that negative interpretations often impose. When you reinterpret setbacks as opportunities, you ease the emotional burden and create space for growth and resilience. This shift in thinking can bring about an emotional uplift, turning what once seemed like a hindrance into a stepping stone. Embracing this mindset doesn't mean ignoring difficulties but instead seeing them as part of a broader narrative where each challenge holds potential for learning and development.

Here are some common negative thoughts that people often struggle with, along with suggestions for how to reframe them:

1. "I'm not good enough."
   - **Reframe:** "I have strengths and areas for improvement. I'm constantly learning and growing."
   - **Action:** List your achievements and qualities you appreciate about yourself.
2. "I always fail at everything."
   - **Reframe:** "Failing is part of the learning process. Every setback teaches me something valuable."
   - **Action:** Reflect on past failures and identify what you learned from each experience.
3. "I'll never be happy."
   - **Reframe:** "Happiness is a journey, and there are small moments of Joy I can find daily."
   - **Action:** start a gratitude journal to focus on positive aspects of your daily life.
4. "I can't handle this."
   - **Reframe:** "This is challenging, but I've faced difficulties before and have the tools to cope."
   - **Action:** Apply coping strategies that have worked for you in the past.
5. "People will think I'm a failure."
   - **Reframe:** "Everyone has struggles, and most people are more understanding than I think."
   - **Action:** Reach out to a friend or mentor for support and perspective.

6. "I always make bad decisions."
   - **Reframe:** "I can learn from my decisions, and I've made good ones in the past."
   - **Action:** Reflect on past decisions where you succeeded and analyze what contributed to those successes.
7. "I'm too old/young to start over."
   - **Reframe:** "It's never too late (or too early) to pursue new goals and dreams."
   - **Action:** Research inspiring stories of people who started new Ventures at different stages of life.
8. "I'm a burden to others."
   - **Reframe:** "My friends and family care about me, and they want to help. It's okay to lean on them."
   - **Action:** "Practice reaching out for support when you're feeling down.
9. "I'm going to embarrass myself."
   - **Reframe:** "Everyone makes mistakes, and it's a natural part of being human. My worth isn't determined by what others think."
   - **Action:** Shift Focus to engaging fully in the moment rather than worrying about potential judgment.
10. "I shouldn't feel this way."
    - **Reframe:** "It's okay to feel this way; emotions are valid and part of being human. I can acknowledge my feelings and work through them."
    - **Action:** Practice mindfulness or journaling to explore your feelings without judgment.

By Consciously reframing these negative thoughts, individuals can shift their mindset toward a more positive and constructive outlook, which can significantly improve their emotional well-being and resilience.

Consider a scenario where you receive criticism at work. Your immediate thought might be, "I'm not good at my job." However, by applying cognitive reframing, you can view this feedback as a chance to improve and grow. Instead of focusing on the negative, acknowledge the opportunity to refine your skills and demonstrate adaptability. This perspective reduces the sting of criticism and empowers you to take constructive action. Similarly, when faced with daily challenges, practice reframing by identifying the silver lining. For instance, a traffic jam might seem frustrating, but it could also be an opportunity to listen to a favorite podcast or enjoy a moment of reflection.

Exercise: Reframing Daily Challenges

At the end of each day, reflect on any challenging situations you faced. Write them down, along with your initial negative interpretation. Then, consciously reframe each situation, focusing on the potential positives or lessons learned. For example, if you missed a deadline, consider what you gained from the experience instead of berating yourself—perhaps better time management skills or a reminder to seek help. Revisit these reflections regularly to reinforce the habit of positive reinterpretation.

By practicing these techniques consistently, cognitive reframing can become a natural part of your thinking process. It empowers you to navigate life's complexities with a more balanced and resilient mindset. Instead of feeling trapped by negative thoughts, you'll find that you have the tools to redefine them, transforming obstacles into opportunities for growth. Each time you reframe an idea, you're not just changing your perspective at that moment; you're building a foundation for more positive and constructive thinking patterns in the future.

2.2 BREAKING THE OVERTHINKING CYCLE

Overthinking can feel like an endless loop, where thoughts swirl uncontrollably, never settling long enough for clarity. It's like being caught in a mental storm, where the noise is overwhelming, and the calm is elusive. Recognizing the triggers that lead to overthinking is crucial in taking control. Common triggers include social interactions and decision-making. You might replay a conversation with a friend, dissect each word for hidden meanings, or agonize over every detail of a decision, fearing the potential outcomes. These scenarios can lead to what's known as analysis paralysis, where the sheer volume of thoughts makes it impossible to decide or move forward. It's as though your mind has built a wall around you, trapping you in indecision and doubt.

The effects of overthinking extend beyond mere frustration. They seep into your emotional well-being, often intensifying anxiety and depression. The constant rumination can lead to emotional exhaustion, leaving you mentally tired and drained. When your mind constantly races, focusing on the present or enjoying life's simple pleasures is challenging. Over time, this relentless cycle can erode your self-confidence and cloud your judgment, making it difficult to trust your instincts or enjoy spontaneous moments. Overthinking can be heavy, casting a shadow over your day-to-day experiences. *Before we move on, please reread this paragraph. It should be reviewed again for clarity and understanding.*

To disrupt the patterns of overthinking, we must break this cycle. Mindfulness meditation offers a powerful tool for anchoring yourself in the present moment. By focusing on your breath or the sensations in your body, you can gently redirect your mind away from the chaos of overthinking. This practice calms the noise and cultivates awareness that helps you recognize when your thoughts start to spiral. Another effective method is scheduling worry time, where you allocate specific periods to reflect on concerns. By setting boundaries around when you allow yourself to worry, you can prevent it from intruding into every aspect of your life, creating a sense of control and balance.

Cultivating a focused mindset requires consistent practice and commitment. Guided visualization techniques can help redirect your thoughts toward more positive and constructive imagery. Imagine a tranquil scene or a place where you feel safe and at ease. This mental escape can provide a much-needed respite from overthinking, offering clarity and calm. Progressive muscle relaxation is another technique that can ease mental tension. You release physical tension by systematically tensing and relaxing different muscle groups, which can also alleviate mental stress. This exercise promotes relaxation and enhances awareness of how your body responds to stress, breaking the cycle of overthinking.

Exercise: Guided Visualization for Mental Clarity

Find a quiet, comfortable space where you can relax. Close your eyes and take a few deep breaths, allowing your body to settle. Visualize a peaceful place that brings you joy and calm, whether a beach, a forest, or a cozy room. Picture every detail—the colors, sounds, and sensations. Let yourself linger in this imagery, noticing how your mind begins to quiet and your body relaxes. Practice this visualization regularly to cultivate a focused and clear mindset.

Breaking the cycle of overthinking is not about eliminating thoughts entirely but about learning to manage them in a way that serves you. By recognizing your triggers and employing strategies like mindfulness and visualization, you can reclaim your mental space, allowing for greater clarity and peace. This journey is about finding balance amidst the chaos, giving yourself the freedom to live more fully and with greater ease.

2.3 TURNING SELF-CRITICISM INTO SELF-COMPASSION

Self-criticism often feels like a relentless inner critic, highlighting every flaw and misstep. That voice in your head never seems satisfied, always pointing out what you could have done better or how you fell short. This focus on imperfections can be debilitating, making it difficult to see your strengths and accomplishments. On the other hand, self-compassion offers a kinder perspective that acknowledges your imperfections but embraces them with understanding and empathy. It's about treating yourself with the same warmth and care you would provide a dear friend. When you shift from criticism to compassion, you create a nurturing space for growth and healing. This change can significantly impact your mental health by reducing stress and fostering a sense of acceptance and peace.

The psychological benefits of self-compassion are profound. You increase your self-esteem and reduce anxiety by cultivating a compassionate inner voice. This approach fosters emotional resilience, helping you bounce back from setbacks with greater ease and adaptability. When you practice self-compassion, you become more attuned to your needs and emotions, enhancing your overall well-being. Research has shown that individuals who practice self-compassion experience less anxiety and depression as they learn to manage their emotions more effectively. This practice encourages a mindset of growth and learning rather than one of failure and inadequacy. By embracing self-compassion, you build a foundation of resilience that supports you through life's challenges.

Several techniques can guide you in cultivating self-compassion. Loving-kindness meditation is a powerful practice that involves directing kind and loving thoughts towards yourself. As you sit quietly, repeat phrases such as "May I be happy" or "May I be at peace." This meditation fosters a sense of warmth and care, gradually replacing harsh self-judgment with kindness. Another technique is the use of daily self-compassion mantras. You can repeat These simple affirmations throughout the day, such as "I am enough" or "I am worthy of love." Integrating these mantras into your routine reinforces a compassionate mindset, making it a natural part of your internal dialogue.

Engaging in practical exercises can further enhance your ability to practice self-compassion. Consider writing a self-compassionate letter. Take a moment to reflect on a situation where you fell short. Write a letter to yourself from the perspective of a supportive friend, acknowledging your feelings and offering words of kindness and encouragement. This exercise allows you to step back from self-criticism and see the situation with greater clarity and compassion. Another way to practice self-compassion is by reframing failures as learning opportunities. Instead of dwelling on what went wrong, focus on what you can learn from the experience. This shift in perspective eases the sting of failure and opens the door to growth and improvement.

By incorporating these practices into your life, you gradually transform your relationship with yourself. Self-compassion becomes a guiding principle that encourages you to approach each day with kindness and understanding. As you nurture this compassionate inner voice, you'll find that it supports you in moments of doubt and difficulty, reassuring you that you are worthy of love and acceptance. This shift from self-criticism to self-compassion is not just a change in mindset; it's a profound transformation that can enhance your mental health and well-being.

2.4 TOOLS FOR EMOTIONAL REGULATION

Managing emotions effectively is like having a compass in a storm, guiding you toward calmer waters and a clearer mind. Emotional regulation plays a vital role in mental health, serving as a buffer against anxiety and depression. Tuning into your emotions and responding productively enables you to handle life's ups and downs more effectively. Rather than being swept away by intense feelings, emotional regulation allows you to pause, reflect, and choose how to react. This ability can significantly improve your well-being, helping you maintain balance even during challenging times.

Several strategies can aid in regulating emotions. Deep breathing exercises are a simple yet powerful tool that can bring immediate calm. By focusing on slow, deliberate breaths, you signal to your body that it's time to relax, which can help alleviate stress and anxiety. Cognitive restructuring offers another avenue, allowing you to alter emotional perceptions by challenging and changing unhelpful thoughts. This technique involves examining the evidence for your thoughts and considering alternative, more balanced perspectives. Over time, it can help shift emotional responses, fostering a sense of control and stability.

Routines play a crucial role in emotional stability. Establishing a structured daily routine can provide predictability, which can be comforting in times of uncertainty. When you know what to expect, you reduce the mental load of constant decision-making, leaving more energy for the things that matter. Whether setting a regular bedtime, scheduling breaks during the day, or planning meals, these routines can anchor you, offering a sense of normalcy and order. By creating predictable patterns, you enhance your ability to manage emotions, making it easier to navigate through the day with greater ease.

To practice emotional regulation, you can engage in exercises that help you identify and process your emotions. Emotion labeling involves recognizing and naming the emotions you're experiencing. By putting your feelings into words, you gain clarity and insight, making it easier to understand what you're going through. Journaling provides a space to explore these emotions further, allowing you to reflect on their causes and effects. Visualization techniques can also be beneficial, helping ground you emotionally. By visualizing a peaceful scene or a comforting memory, you can transport yourself to a calm place, reducing the intensity of overwhelming emotions.

Exercise: Visualization for Emotional Grounding

Find a quiet space and sit comfortably. Close your eyes and take a few deep breaths, allowing your body to relax. Picture a place where you feel safe and at peace. It could be a serene beach, a cozy room, or a lush forest. Focus on the details— the colors, sounds, and sensations—and fully immerse yourself in this visualization. Notice how your body responds, feeling lighter and more grounded. Practice this technique whenever you feel emotionally unsettled to bring yourself back to a place of calm and balance.

These tools for emotional regulation are not about suppressing emotions but rather about managing them in a way that supports your mental health. These strategies allow you to navigate emotional challenges with greater resilience and confidence. As you continue to develop these skills, you'll find that they become second nature, helping you maintain emotional equilibrium even in the face of stress. Understanding and applying these techniques allows you to take charge of your emotional well-being, paving the way for a more balanced and fulfilling life.

With a foundation in emotional regulation, you are well-prepared to explore the next chapter, which delves into practical CBT techniques for everyday anxiety. These strategies will build on your knowledge, offering more tools to enhance your mental health and resilience.

3

PRACTICAL CBT TECHNIQUES FOR EVERYDAY ANXIETY

Picture this: you're standing in the middle of a bustling shopping mall, surrounded by a sea of people. Conversations blend into a chaotic noise, and the bright lights seem to intensify your growing anxiety. Your heart races, your palms sweat, and every instinct urges you to escape. In moments like these, grounding techniques become invaluable tools. Grounding is the practice of anchoring yourself in the present moment by focusing on external stimuli to manage anxiety, pulling you away from overwhelming feelings, and helping you regain a sense of control. By engaging your senses, grounding techniques can interrupt the cycle of anxious thoughts that often spiral out of control, providing a lifeline when needed.

One powerful physical grounding exercise is the **5-4-3-2-1** sensory technique. This method involves using your senses to connect with the world around you. Begin by identifying **five things** you can see, such as a colorful sign or a passerby's hat. Next, focus on **four things** you can touch, like the softness of your sweater or the coolness of a nearby bench. Then, tune into **three sounds**, whether the hum of conversation or the rustle of shopping bags. Follow this by noticing **two scents**, such as freshly brewed coffee or the perfume of someone passing by. Finally, identify **one thing** you can taste, perhaps a lingering mint from earlier. This exercise engages your senses, drawing your attention away from anxiety and back to the present.

Progressive muscle relaxation (PMR) offers another effective way to ground yourself physically. This technique involves tensing and slowly releasing different muscle groups to ease tension and stress. Begin by sitting comfortably and taking a deep breath. Start with your toes, curling them tightly, then releasing. Move up to your calves, tightening them and then letting go. Continue this pattern through your body—thighs, abdomen, chest, arms, and neck—focusing on the sensation of tension melting away. PMR calms the body and redirects your focus, providing relief from anxious thoughts.

Mental grounding strategies can also divert attention from anxiety. Counting backward from 100 in sevens is a cognitive exercise that requires concentration, which can help disrupt the flow of worrisome thoughts. Similarly, reciting a favorite poem or song lyrics engages your mind, creating a mental anchor and stabilizing your emotions. By focusing on familiar words or numbers, you occupy your mind with something tangible and predictable, easing the intensity of anxiety.

Guided visualizations can provide a mental escape, offering a soothing retreat from distressing environments. Imagine yourself in a serene meadow, the sun warming your skin and a gentle breeze rustling the grass. Visualize the colors, sounds, and sensations, immersing yourself in this peaceful scene. This practice can transport you to a calm place, even amidst chaos. Picture using this visualization technique while waiting in a crowded doctor's office, the chatter around you fading as you focus on the tranquility of your imagined sanctuary.

In crowded environments, grounding can be beneficial. Picture yourself navigating a packed subway station. The noise and movement can trigger anxiety, making it difficult to breathe. In such moments, grounding provides a refuge. Focus on the texture of the railing you're holding, the rhythmic sound of the train approaching, or the cool air against your skin. These sensory details offer a tangible connection to the present, breaking the hold of anxiety. As you practice these grounding techniques, you'll find they become second nature, equipping you with a reliable toolkit to manage anxiety wherever and whenever it arises.

Exercise: Sensory Grounding Practice

Pause for a moment to engage in the 5-4-3-2-1 grounding exercise. Find a spot where you can sit comfortably and gently close your eyes. Begin to consciously connect with your environment through each of your senses, carefully observing the details around you. Note the shift in your focus from internal anxieties to the present moment. Document your experiences and thoughts on how this technique impacts your feeling of tranquility. Grounding techniques are invaluable, not solely as immediate responses to anxiety but as everyday practices that enhance life's quality.

Regularly incorporating these practices into your daily routine lays down the pillars of resilience, equipping you to approach life's varied challenges with assurance and tranquility.

3.1 MANAGING SOCIAL ANXIETY IN PUBLIC SETTINGS

Social anxiety often finds its roots in situations where you feel exposed or vulnerable to judgment. Imagine standing at a podium, about to present to your colleagues, or entering a bustling party where you know only a handful of faces. These scenarios can trigger a cascade of anxious thoughts and physical symptoms, making it challenging to engage fully. Public speaking at work or school, for instance, is a common source of anxiety. The fear of stumbling over words or being judged harshly can feel overwhelming, leading to avoidance or distress. Similarly, attending large social gatherings can provoke anxiety as you're faced with the prospect of navigating conversations and social cues amidst a crowd. The mere anticipation of such events can set your heart racing as your mind conjures up worst-case scenarios where you might embarrass yourself or fail to connect with others.

Cognitive Behavioral Therapy (CBT) offers several techniques to help manage social anxiety, providing a structured approach to tackle these fears. One effective method is role-playing, where you rehearse social interactions beforehand. This practice involves simulating conversations or presentations with a trusted friend or therapist, allowing you to anticipate potential challenges and responses. Doing so can build confidence and reduce the unpredictability of actual interactions. Another powerful tool is cognitive restructuring, which helps you challenge negative assumptions about yourself and others. For example, suppose you believe people will judge you harshly at a party. In that case, cognitive restructuring encourages you to examine the evidence for this belief and consider alternative, less threatening interpretations. This shift in perspective can alleviate anxiety, making social situations feel less daunting.

Exposure therapy, a core component of CBT, involves gradually facing your fears to diminish their power. Start with small, manageable social interactions, such as chatting with a familiar colleague or attending a small gathering. As you become more comfortable, gradually increase the complexity and size of the settings. This might mean introducing yourself to a new group at a networking event or participating in a larger social gathering. By exposing yourself to these situations in a controlled and supportive manner, you can desensitize your anxiety over time. This process reduces avoidance behaviors and builds resilience, empowering you to handle increasingly challenging social contexts with greater ease and confidence.

Real-life examples can illustrate these strategies in action. Consider Sarah, who once avoided networking events due to overwhelming anxiety. Through CBT, she began role-playing interactions with her therapist, practicing introducing herself and engaging in small talk. This preparation helped her approach her first networking event more confidently, focusing on the skills she had honed rather than her fears. Similarly, Mark struggled with crowds and often felt paralyzed in busy environments like concerts or festivals. By gradually exposing himself to smaller crowds and using cognitive restructuring to challenge his assumptions about others' judgments, his anxiety lessened over time. These narratives highlight the transformative potential of CBT techniques, demonstrating how targeted strategies can lead to meaningful change.

By applying these CBT techniques, you can learn to manage social anxiety more effectively, allowing you to engage with the world on your terms. The journey to overcoming social anxiety is not without its challenges. Still, with persistence and practice, it is possible to navigate public settings more confidently and efficiently.

3.2 CBT STRATEGIES FOR WORKPLACE STRESS

Workplace stress, a common challenge, arises from professional pressures and demands. Looming deadlines and growing workloads can be overwhelming, fostering feelings of inadequacy and fear of failure that hinder performance. Interpersonal conflicts introduce further tension, complicating the work environment. Effective strategies are essential for managing stress and restoring control to navigate these issues peacefully.

Cognitive Behavioral Therapy (CBT) offers practical tools to manage workplace stress, beginning with time management techniques. Prioritizing tasks can help reduce the anxiety that comes with looming deadlines. Start by identifying the most urgent and vital tasks, breaking them into smaller, manageable steps. This approach makes the workload less daunting and provides a clear roadmap for getting things done. Additionally, setting realistic goals and deadlines can prevent the stress of unmet expectations. It's essential to remember that not everything needs to be perfect; sometimes, good enough is indeed good enough. By practicing time management, you can alleviate the pressure of deadlines, allowing you to approach your work with a renewed sense of focus and energy.

Assertiveness training is another effective CBT strategy for handling workplace conflicts. It involves learning to communicate your needs and boundaries clearly and respectfully. This skill is crucial in managing interpersonal relationships, as it empowers you to express yourself without aggression or passivity. For example, if a colleague's behavior is causing stress, you might say, "I've noticed that our communication could be clearer. Can we discuss how to improve it?" This approach fosters a more collaborative environment, reducing tension and promoting mutual understanding. Assertiveness training can help you navigate workplace politics, ensuring your voice is heard and respected.

Cognitive restructuring is pivotal in managing stress by altering how you perceive challenges and setbacks. When faced with a daunting project, your initial thought might be, "I'll never get this done." This negative mindset can fuel stress and anxiety, making it harder to focus and perform. Cognitive restructuring encourages you to challenge and replace these thoughts with more balanced ones. For instance, you might reframe the idea to, "This project is challenging, but I can tackle it step by step." This shift in perspective can alleviate the pressure, allowing you to approach your work confidently and clearly.

Incorporating mindful breathing during breaks can provide a much-needed mental reset amidst the hustle and bustle of the workday. Taking a few moments to focus on your breath can calm the mind and body, reducing stress and enhancing concentration. Visualization techniques can also be beneficial, especially before stressful meetings or presentations. Picture yourself succeeding, speaking clearly, and engaging positively with others. This mental rehearsal can boost your self-assurance, making daunting tasks feel more manageable.

Consider the scenario of a project manager overwhelmed by a looming deadline and a team struggling with communication. By applying CBT strategies, they prioritize tasks and set a realistic timeline, easing the burden of urgency. Assertiveness training helps them address team dynamics, fostering a more supportive and efficient work environment. Through cognitive restructuring, they transform their negative self-talk into constructive reflections, viewing challenges as opportunities for growth. Mindful breathing and visualization techniques become their allies, grounding them in moments of stress and preparing them for success. These strategies reduce workplace stress and enhance overall well-being, empowering them to thrive professionally and personally.

3.3 CALMING THE MIND BEFORE SLEEP

As the day winds down, anxiety often finds its way into the quiet moments before sleep. No longer distracted by the day's activities, the mind can become a breeding ground for racing thoughts. These thoughts swirl relentlessly, making it challenging to find peace. You might find yourself replaying the day's events, worrying about tomorrow's challenges, or imagining worst-case scenarios. This mental chatter can interfere with your ability to fall asleep and stay asleep, contributing to insomnia. The cycle is frustrating and exhausting, leaving you feeling drained each morning. Anxiety-induced insomnia is more than just a nuisance; it can affect your overall well-being, impacting your mood, concentration, and physical health.

Cognitive Behavioral Therapy offers practical techniques to help calm the mind before bed to combat this. Establishing a sleep hygiene routine is a crucial first step. This involves creating a series of habits that signal your body that it's time to wind down. Start by setting a consistent bedtime and wake-up time, even on weekends. This routine helps regulate your body's internal clock, making it easier to fall asleep and wake up naturally. Limit exposure to screens at least an hour before bed, as the blue light emitted can interfere with your body's production of melatonin, the sleep hormone. Engage in calming activities, such as reading a book or taking a warm bath, to help your body transition to a restful state.

Relaxation techniques, such as guided imagery and deep breathing, can further ease nighttime anxiety. Guided imagery involves visualizing a peaceful scene in your mind, such as a tranquil beach or a serene forest. Focus on the details—the sound of waves, the sun's warmth, the scent of pine. This mental escape can help distract your mind from anxious thoughts, allowing relaxation to take hold. Deep breathing, on the other hand, slows your heart rate and calms your nervous system. Try inhaling deeply through your nose for four counts, holding for seven, and exhaling slowly through your mouth for eight. This rhythmic breathing can help you release tension and enter a state of calm.

Cognitive restructuring plays a pivotal role in addressing anxiety at bedtime. The thoughts that keep you awake are often catastrophic, amplifying your worries. You might fear you'll fail at work or let others down if you don't sleep enough. Cognitive restructuring encourages you to challenge these thoughts by examining their validity. Ask yourself, "What evidence do I have that supports this fear?" and "What would I say to a friend with this thought?" Reframing these fears can reduce their power, easing the anxiety that keeps you awake.

Incorporating exercises and bedtime routines can further support relaxation and improve sleep quality. Start by creating a sleep-inducing environment. Ensure your bedroom is cool, dark, and quiet. Use blackout curtains, earplugs, or a white noise machine to eliminate distractions. If your mind tends to race with worries, try journaling before bed. Write down your concerns and possible solutions or steps you can take tomorrow. This practice can help clear your mind, allowing you to let go of the day's stressors. As you crawl into bed, remind yourself that you've done what you can for today, and tomorrow is a new opportunity.

These techniques can transform your bedtime experience, making it a peaceful transition rather than a nightly struggle. As you practice these methods, your sleep improves, leaving you feeling more refreshed and ready to face each day. Sleep is not just a necessity; it's a foundation for mental and emotional resilience. By calming your mind before bed, you give yourself the gift of rest, which can profoundly impact your overall well-being.

3.4 OVERCOMING FEAR OF JUDGMENT

Fear of judgment can feel like a constant shadow, lurking in every interaction and influencing how you present yourself to the world. This fear often stems from past experiences and self-esteem issues. A critical comment from a teacher or peer in your formative years planted seeds of doubt, or a significant setback left a lasting impression. These experiences shape our perceptions of how others see us, often leading us to assume the worst. We believe others constantly evaluate us, ready to highlight our flaws. This mindset can paralyze us, making us hesitant to express ourselves fully or take risks. Over time, the fear of judgment can become a barrier, preventing us from engaging with the world as our true selves.

Cognitive Behavioral Therapy (CBT) offers practical methods to address this fear, starting with cognitive restructuring. This technique involves challenging the beliefs you hold about others' perceptions. You might think, "If I speak up, they'll think I'm foolish." CBT encourages you to question this assumption: What evidence supports this thought? Is there a chance you're projecting your insecurities onto others? By dissecting these beliefs, you can see that they often lack a solid foundation. Building self-confidence through positive affirmations is another powerful tool. By repeating phrases like "I am capable and worthy of respect," you can gradually shift your internal narrative. This practice helps reinforce a positive self-image, reducing the weight of external judgments.

Exposure techniques specifically tailored to the fear of judgment can also be transformative. Start small by practicing conversations with strangers in low-stakes environments, like a café or bookstore. Engage in small talk, focusing on the interaction rather than the fear of judgment. Gradual exposure helps desensitize you to the anxiety of being evaluated. As you become more comfortable, the complexity of these interactions increases. This might mean sharing your opinions in a group setting or leading a meeting at work. With each step, you build resilience, proving that you can navigate these situations without succumbing to fear.

Consider the example of a person who once dreaded public speaking. This fear of judgment kept them silent in meetings despite having valuable insights to share. CBT taught them to challenge their assumptions, realizing that colleagues valued their contributions. They began practicing small presentations, gradually increasing their confidence. Over time, they overcame their fear and became a sought-after speaker within their team. This transformation wasn't overnight, but they redefined their relationship with judgment through persistence and practice.

Exercises focusing on self-validation can further support this journey. Create a list of personal achievements and strengths. Reflect on them regularly, especially when self-doubt creeps in. This practice reminds you of your capabilities and worth, reinforcing a positive self-concept. Building resilience requires patience and compassion towards yourself. Each step you take towards confronting the fear of judgment is a victory, no matter how small.

As you work through these techniques, remember that you're not alone. Many people grapple with fear of judgment, and it's a challenge that can be overcome with time and effort. Embracing these strategies opens the door to greater freedom and authenticity. You learn to trust yourself, valuing your opinions and abilities over others' perceptions. This empowerment is not just about silencing the fear of judgment; it's about finding your voice and using it confidently in any situation.

4

ENHANCING EMOTIONAL RESILIENCE

I magine a tree standing tall in a storm. Its branches sway wildly, but the roots hold firm, grounding it against the fiercest winds. This image captures the essence of emotional resilience—your ability to withstand and recover from life's challenges. Emotional resilience is the capacity to bounce back from adversity, adapt to change, and keep moving forward despite setbacks. It's not about avoiding difficulties but facing them with strength and grace. In maintaining mental health, resilience acts as a buffer, protecting against the ravages of stress and anxiety and fostering a sense of hope and empowerment.

Cognitive Behavioral Therapy (CBT) is pivotal in building resilience by equipping you with tools to navigate life's challenges. Through cognitive restructuring, you learn to identify and alter negative thought patterns, fostering adaptive thinking that enhances your ability to cope with stress. This technique involves examining your beliefs and assumptions, challenging unhelpful ones, and replacing them with more constructive alternatives. For example, instead of viewing a setback as a personal failure, you might reframe it as a learning opportunity, reinforcing the belief that growth is possible even in adversity. This shift in perspective can strengthen your resilience, making it easier to face challenges with courage and optimism.

Behavioral experiments are another powerful CBT strategy for building resilience. These experiments involve testing your beliefs through real-world actions to gather evidence that challenges your assumptions. Suppose you believe that asking for help will burden others. A behavioral experiment might involve requesting assistance with a task and observing the response. Often, you'll find that people are more willing to help than anticipated, which can alter your belief and increase your confidence in seeking support. This practice builds resilience by challenging limiting beliefs. It enhances problem-solving abilities, helping you navigate life's complexities more easily.

Resilience offers numerous benefits in daily life, improving your ability to manage stress and enhancing problem-solving skills. When you're resilient, you are better equipped to handle the pressures of work, relationships, and personal challenges. Stressful situations become more manageable as you develop the capacity to remain calm and focused even amidst chaos. This improved stress management can enhance performance and satisfaction in various areas of your life. Solving problems effectively also improves, as resilience fosters creativity and flexibility, allowing you to approach challenges from different angles and find innovative solutions.

To cultivate resilience, consider integrating daily reflection journals into your routine. Each day, take a few moments to reflect on your experiences, noting any challenges you faced and how you responded. This practice encourages self-awareness and helps you identify patterns in your thoughts and behaviors that may affect your resilience. By reflecting on your experiences, you can learn from them, recognizing areas where you demonstrated resilience and opportunities for growth. This self-reflection fosters a more profound understanding of your strengths and areas for improvement, empowering you to build resilience over time.

Scenario analysis is another practical exercise for enhancing resilience. This technique involves examining past challenges and analyzing how you handled them. Consider a problematic situation and dissect the steps you took to navigate it. What strategies did you use? What worked well, and what could you have done differently? By analyzing experiences, you gain insights into your resilience strategies, allowing you to refine and strengthen them for future challenges. This analysis enhances your self-awareness and builds confidence in overcoming adversity.

Exercise: Resilience Reflection Journal

Dedicate a few minutes each day to writing in your resilience reflection journal. Note any challenges you faced, your initial reactions, and the strategies you used to cope. Reflect on what you learned from the experience and how it strengthened your resilience. Use these reflections to identify patterns and areas for growth, reinforcing your resilience over time.

As you practice these exercises, you cultivate a resilient mindset that empowers you to thrive in the face of adversity. Resilience is not a fixed trait but a skill that can be developed and strengthened with practice. By incorporating these strategies into your daily life, you build a foundation of resilience that supports you through life's challenges, fostering a sense of hope and empowerment.

4.1 THE ART OF BOUNCING BACK: LEARNING FROM SETBACKS

Consider setbacks as stepping stones rather than stumbling blocks. Each challenge presents a chance to grow, reshape perspectives, and develop resilience. When we embrace this mindset, setbacks transform into valuable lessons that propel us forward. This approach, known as a growth mindset, encourages you to see challenges as opportunities for development rather than insurmountable obstacles. Shifting your view empowers you to learn and adapt rather than feel defeated. This mindset fosters a sense of curiosity and exploration, urging you to ask, "What can I learn from this?" rather than "Why did this happen to me?" It's a subtle but powerful change in how you perceive and respond to life's inevitable hurdles.

Constructively analyzing setbacks is essential for learning from them. Reflective journaling is a practical tool for processing and assessing your experiences. By writing about a setback, you gain clarity on the emotions and thoughts it triggered. This practice helps you identify patterns and root causes, offering insights into how you can approach similar situations differently in the future. Additionally, identifying lessons and strategies for future challenges can turn a setback into a roadmap for success. Consider what worked, what didn't, and how you might adjust your approach next time. This reflection encourages growth and prepares you for future challenges, reinforcing that setbacks are not failures but opportunities for refinement and improvement.

Self-compassion plays a vital role in bouncing back from setbacks. It's about treating yourself with the same kindness and understanding you would offer a friend facing a similar situation. Practicing self-forgiveness and understanding is crucial during these times. Acknowledge that everyone makes mistakes and faces difficulties. Being gentle with yourself creates a supportive environment for recovery, allowing you to move forward without the burden of guilt or shame. This self-kindness fosters resilience, encouraging you to see setbacks as part of the human experience rather than personal shortcomings. Embracing self-compassion is a powerful step toward healing and growth, as it nurtures a mindset of acceptance and hope.

Consider the story of an entrepreneur who faced significant business failures. Initially, the challenges seemed impossible, leading to doubt and frustration. However, embracing a growth mindset, they began viewing each failure as a learning opportunity. Through reflective journaling, they identified key lessons and strategies for future endeavors. This process helped them bounce back stronger and fueled their innovation and creativity. By practicing self-compassion, they forgave themselves for past mistakes, allowing them to focus on future possibilities rather than dwelling on what went wrong. This narrative illustrates the power of reframing setbacks as opportunities for growth, highlighting how resilience can lead to success and fulfillment.

Exercise: Writing a Personal Narrative of Resilience

Take a moment to reflect on a recent setback. Write a personal narrative describing the experience, focusing on the emotions, thoughts, and actions involved. Identify key lessons learned and consider how you might approach similar challenges differently in the future. Practice self-compassion by acknowledging your efforts and growth, recognizing that setbacks are stepping stones on your path to resilience.

Remember that setbacks are not definitive failures when engaging with these concepts and exercises. They are opportunities to build resilience and develop a deeper understanding of yourself. By embracing a growth mindset, practicing self-compassion, and reflecting on your experiences, you empower yourself to bounce back stronger and more resilient than before.

4.2 CBT EXERCISES FOR STRENGTHENING RESILIENCE

Building emotional resilience takes practice and intention. The ABC model, a cornerstone of Cognitive Behavioral Therapy, is a great place to start. This model breaks down experiences into three parts:

1. **The activating event,**
2. **The Belief about the event,**
3. **The Consequence of that belief.**

For example, suppose you receive criticism at work (Activating event). In that case, you might believe, "I'm not good enough" (Belief), leading to feelings of inadequacy and withdrawal (Consequence). By examining and altering these beliefs, you can change the emotional fallout. Instead of thinking negatively, you might reframe the belief to, "I can learn from this feedback," which fosters a more positive and resilient response.

Behavioral activation is another powerful exercise to confront avoidance and build resilience. When faced with stress, it's natural to withdraw or avoid challenging situations. However, this can reinforce negative patterns and erode resilience. Behavioral activation encourages you to engage in activities that align with your values and goals, even when you don't feel like it. Start small—perhaps by taking a short walk or contacting a friend. Gradually, you can build up to more challenging activities. This practice boosts your mood and enhances your ability to face difficult situations with courage and determination.

Exposure therapy is a method within CBT that involves gradually confronting fears to build emotional strength. By exposing yourself to anxiety-inducing situations in a controlled way, you can reduce their power over you. Begin with less daunting scenarios and work your way up. If social situations are anxiety-provoking, start by practicing conversations with a trusted friend and then progress to attending a social event. The goal is not to eliminate fear but to increase your tolerance and confidence. This gradual exposure helps you develop resilience, allowing you to navigate challenges more efficiently and assuredly.

Cognitive restructuring exercises are essential for challenging and changing maladaptive beliefs undermining resilience. Thought record sheets can be a helpful tool in this process. You can analyze the underlying beliefs by documenting situations that trigger negative thoughts. This practice involves identifying evidence for and against these beliefs, exploring alternative interpretations, and considering each perspective's emotional and behavioral consequences. This exercise teaches you to question and reframe unhelpful thoughts, replacing them with more balanced and constructive ones. Over time, this skill strengthens your resilience, empowering you to face life's difficulties with a more precise and positive mindset.

Integrating these exercises into your life requires structure and consistency. Creating a weekly resilience-building schedule can help you stay on track. Dedicate specific times each week to practice the ABC model, engage in behavioral activation, and use thought record sheets. This routine reinforces these practices and helps you track progress and adjust your approach. Self-assessment is a valuable part of this process, allowing you to reflect on your growth, identify areas for improvement, and celebrate your successes. By regularly evaluating your resilience-building efforts, you maintain momentum and motivation, ensuring these exercises become a natural and enduring part of your life.

These CBT exercises offer a toolkit for building resilience, providing the skills to face life's challenges with confidence and strength. As you engage with these practices, remember that resilience is not about never falling but about rising each time you do. By incorporating these exercises into your life, you cultivate a resilient mindset that empowers you to thrive amidst adversity.

4.3 CULTIVATING A POSITIVE MINDSET

Imagine seeing the world through a lens that highlights opportunities rather than obstacles. This is the power of a positive mindset. It's not about ignoring difficulties but focusing on their possibilities. Positivity plays a crucial role in emotional resilience, acting as a catalyst for problem-solving skills. When faced with a challenge, a positive mindset allows you to approach it with curiosity and creativity. Instead of feeling stuck, you see multiple paths forward. This optimistic outlook enhances your ability to devise practical solutions and adapt to changing circumstances. By cultivating positivity, you empower yourself to tackle problems head-on, transforming potential roadblocks into stepping-stones.

There are several techniques you can use to foster a more positive outlook. Gratitude journaling is a simple yet profound practice that shifts your focus to the positive aspects of life. Take a moment to jot down three things you're grateful for daily. They can be big or small—a kind gesture from a friend, a beautiful sunset, or the satisfaction of completing a task. Over time, this practice trains your brain to notice and appreciate the good around you, fostering a sense of contentment and well-being. Positive visualization is another technique that can enhance your mindset. Spend a few minutes each day visualizing yourself achieving your goals. Picture the steps you'll take, the obstacles you'll overcome, and the joy of success. These visualizations can boost your motivation and confidence, making your aspirations feel within reach.

Maintaining positivity in challenging situations requires conscious effort and practice. One effective strategy is reframing negative thoughts into positive affirmations. When faced with a setback, your mind might default to negative self-talk, like, "I can't do this." Instead, challenge that thought by affirming, "I have the skills and determination to figure this out." This simple shift in language reinforces your belief in your abilities, helping you stay focused and optimistic even in adversity. Positive affirmations are like mental anchors, grounding you in a mindset of possibility and resilience. Regularly practicing this technique trains your mind to default to positivity, building a reservoir of strength to draw upon in difficult times.

To illustrate the power of a positive mindset, consider a scenario where a project at work doesn't go as planned. Instead of viewing it as a failure, you can transform it into a success story by focusing on what you learned and how you grew from the experience. Perhaps you discovered new skills, forged stronger relationships with colleagues, or gained valuable insights for future projects. This reframing not only eases the sting of disappointment but also highlights the growth and progress that emerged from the challenge. Such stories remind you that setbacks are not dead ends but opportunities for development and achievement.

Exercise: Creating Positivity Prompts for Daily Reflection

Take a few moments to create a list of positive prompts you can reflect on daily. These prompts might include questions like, "What went well today?" or "What am I looking forward to tomorrow?" Place these prompts somewhere visible, like your journal or phone, and use them to guide your reflections each day. By focusing on these questions, you encourage a habit of positivity, reinforcing a mindset that seeks out the good in every situation.

By integrating these techniques into your life, you cultivate a positive mindset that supports emotional resilience. This mindset becomes a powerful ally, helping you navigate life's challenges with grace and courage. As you practice these strategies, you'll find that positivity isn't just a fleeting feeling; it's a way of being that transforms how you interact with the world.

4.4 DEVELOPING LONG-TERM RESILIENCE HABITS

Building resilience is akin to nurturing a garden, requiring consistent care and attention. Just as plants rely on routine watering and sunlight, resilience thrives on regular habits that support emotional strength and stability. Long-term resilience helps sustain your ability to bounce back from life's challenges. These habits create a foundation of stability, providing the steady ground needed to weather storms. Routine plays a pivotal role in maintaining resilience, offering predictability and structure that can be comforting in uncertain times. By embedding resilience practices into your daily life, you cultivate a mindset that naturally leans towards growth and adaptability, reinforcing your ability to handle stress and adversity.

One effective resilience-building strategy is incorporating daily rituals promoting reflection and mindfulness. Meditation can be a powerful tool in this regard, offering a moment of calm and introspection amidst the chaos of everyday life. Setting aside time each day to meditate creates a space to reconnect with yourself, fostering a sense of peace and clarity. Similarly, taking time for reflection allows you to process your experiences, identify patterns, and gain insights into your thoughts and emotions. These rituals anchor you and enhance your resilience by encouraging a deeper connection with your inner self. Over time, these practices become second nature, providing a constant source of strength and stability.

Setting resilience goals and milestones further supports the development of long-term habits. By defining specific objectives, you create a roadmap for your growth, offering direction and motivation. These goals include learning a new skill, improving emotional regulation, or building stronger relationships. As you achieve each milestone, you reinforce your commitment to resilience, celebrating your progress and strengthening your belief in your ability to overcome challenges. This process boosts your confidence and encourages continuous growth and improvement, ensuring that resilience remains a central aspect of your life.

Community and support are vital components in sustaining resilience. Building a network of supportive individuals can provide encouragement and motivation, offering a safety net during difficult times. Whether it's friends, family, or support groups, having people to lean on can make a significant difference in your resilience journey. These connections provide a sense of belonging and shared understanding, reminding you that you are not alone in your struggles. By surrounding yourself with positive influences, you create an environment that nurtures resilience, offering guidance and support when needed.

Integrating resilience habits into your life requires a practical plan. Consider setting monthly resilience habit challenges, where you focus on developing a specific habit or skill. For example, dedicate a month to expanding your communication skills or practicing gratitude daily. These challenges encourage experimentation and growth, allowing you to explore different aspects of resilience. Regularly assess your progress and adjust as needed as you face these challenges. Self-assessment is a crucial part of this process, helping you identify areas for improvement and recognize your successes. By regularly evaluating your resilience habits, you maintain momentum and motivation, ensuring these practices become an enduring part of your life.

These strategies offer a framework for developing long-term resilience habits, empowering you to build strength and adaptability. By incorporating these practices into your daily life, you create a resilient mindset that supports you through life's challenges, fostering a sense of hope and empowerment. As you continue this path, you'll find that resilience is not just a skill but a way of being, guiding you toward a life of growth and fulfillment.

In the next chapter, we will explore how integrating Cognitive Behavioral Therapy with holistic health practices can further enhance mental well-being, offering a comprehensive approach to managing anxiety and depression.

5

INTEGRATING CBT WITH
HOLISTIC HEALTH PRACTICES

The first time I sat in quiet contemplation, focusing solely on my breath, it felt like I'd stepped onto a path I hadn't known existed. This practice of mindfulness opened a doorway to a place of calm and clarity within myself, one where anxiety's grip loosened, and my mind could rest. Mindfulness, like Cognitive Behavioral Therapy (CBT), is a powerful tool that can transform how you navigate your mental landscape. Mindfulness enhances CBT's effectiveness by fostering present-moment awareness, offering more profound insights into your thoughts and emotions. This integration creates a

Mindfulness is about being fully present and aware of where you are and what you're doing without being overly reactive or overwhelmed by what's happening around you. It's acknowledging your thoughts and feelings without judgment, seeing them as passing clouds rather than storms. This practice encourages you to observe your experiences with curiosity and openness, allowing you to accept them. By cultivating this awareness, you learn to step back from automatic reactions, creating space to respond with intention and clarity. This shift in perspective can be empowering, reducing the hold on negative thought patterns and enhancing your ability to manage stress and anxiety.

Incorporating mindfulness into CBT offers numerous benefits. It can significantly enhance your focus and attention, helping you fully engage in daily activities. This increased awareness allows you to notice and address emotional triggers before they escalate, fostering better emotional regulation. Mindfulness also cultivates a sense of calm and balance, reducing stress and anxiety. By grounding you in the present moment, it helps you break free from the cycle of rumination and worry that often accompanies anxiety and depression. This practice encourages a more compassionate relationship with yourself, promoting acceptance and understanding.

Several mindfulness techniques align beautifully with CBT, offering practical exercises to support your mental health journey. Mindful breathing is a foundational practice that helps anchor your thoughts. By focusing on the rhythm of your breath, you create a steady point of focus that can calm a racing mind. This practice encourages you to return to your breath whenever you feel overwhelmed, providing a simple yet effective tool for managing stress. Body scan meditation is another technique that connects you with your physical sensations, promoting relaxation and awareness. You can release tension and cultivate a sense of grounding by systematically focusing on each body part.

Consider Sarah, who struggled with anxiety during CBT sessions. By integrating mindfulness, she learned to tune into her breath whenever her thoughts began to spiral. This practice allowed her to stay present, engage more fully in therapy, and gain profound insights into her thought patterns. Similarly, David found that mindfulness helped him manage panic attacks. By practicing body scan meditation, he could focus on his sensations, easing the intensity of his anxiety and regaining control. These examples illustrate the power of mindfulness in action, showing how it can enhance the effectiveness of CBT and support emotional well-being.

Exercise: Mindful Breathing Practice

Set aside a few minutes each day to practice mindful breathing. Find a quiet place to sit comfortably, close your eyes, and focus on your breath. Notice the sensation of the air as it enters and leaves your body. If your mind wanders, gently bring your attention back to your breath. Reflect on how this practice influences your sense of calm and presence. Write down your observations and consider incorporating this exercise into your daily routine.

By weaving mindfulness into your CBT practice, you create a powerful combination that supports emotional resilience and well-being. This integration fosters a more in-depth understanding of yourself and your experiences, empowering you to navigate life's challenges with grace and clarity. As you engage with these practices, remember that mindfulness is not about achieving a state of calm but about embracing the present moment with openness and acceptance.

5.1 COMBINING NUTRITION AND CBT FOR MENTAL HEALTH

Reflecting on the times I felt mentally foggy or emotionally depleted, I began to notice a pattern linked to what I was eating. It became clear that nutrition plays a pivotal role in mental health, influencing mood and cognitive function. The brain, a complex organ, requires a steady supply of nutrients to function optimally. For instance, foods rich in omega-3 fatty acids and magnesium support brain health. Omega-3s in fatty fishlike salmon maintain brain structure and function. At the same time, magnesium, present in nuts and leafy greens, helps regulate neurotransmitters that influence mood. These nutrients act as building blocks, fortifying your brain against the stresses of daily life.

Incorporating nutrition into a Cognitive Behavioral Therapy (CBT) regimen can enhance effectiveness. A balanced diet works hand in hand with CBT by stabilizing mood through balanced blood sugar levels. When blood sugar levels are erratic, it can lead to mood swings and irritability, hindering cognitive processing and emotional regulation. Consuming meals rich in complex carbohydrates, proteins, and healthy fats provides sustained energy and helps maintain equilibrium. Proper nutrition enhances cognitive function, ensuring your mind is sharp and receptive to CBT strategies. By nourishing your body, you create a solid foundation for mental resilience, making it easier to apply CBT techniques effectively.

To support mental well-being through diet, consider incorporating anti-inflammatory foods such as berries and leafy greens into your meals. These foods are rich in antioxidants, which protect the brain from oxidative stress and inflammation, which are linked to mood disorders. Reducing the intake of processed foods and sugars is equally essential, as these can contribute to inflammation and negatively impact mental health. A diet high in refined sugars has been associated with impaired brain function and worsened mood disorders, including depression. You can nurture your body and mind by choosing whole, unprocessed foods, creating a harmonious balance that supports emotional well-being.

Take, for example, a patient who experienced significant improvements in mental health after making dietary changes alongside CBT. Struggling with anxiety and mood fluctuations, they decided to overhaul their eating habits, focusing on whole foods and eliminating processed sugars. Within weeks, they noticed a marked improvement in energy levels and mood stability, which allowed them to engage more fully in CBT sessions. This transformation underscores the powerful impact nutrition can have when combined with therapeutic practices. Meal planning can further support this integration, providing structure and consistency. By preparing nutrient-rich meals ahead of time, you reduce the temptation to reach for convenient but unhealthy options, ensuring your body receives the nourishment it needs to thrive.

Reflection Section: Meal Planning for Mental Health

Consider setting aside time each week to plan and prepare meals that align with your nutritional goals. Focus on incorporating whole foods, emphasizing fruits, vegetables, lean proteins, and healthy fats. Reflect on how these changes affect your mood and cognitive function and note any improvements in your ability to engage with CBT techniques. This proactive approach to nutrition can be a powerful ally in your mental health journey.

By embracing the connection between nutrition and mental health, you empower yourself to make choices that support your physical and emotional well-being. Integrating a balanced diet with CBT practices can create a synergistic effect, enhancing the benefits of each approach. As you nurture your body with the nutrients it craves, you lay the groundwork for a healthier, more resilient mind.

5.2 EXERCISE AND ITS IMPACT ON ANXIETY AND DEPRESSION

I remember a time when my mind felt like a tangled ball of yarn, thoughts looping endlessly, creating knots of anxiety. It was during this phase that I discovered the transformative power of exercise. Physical activity became a release, a way to untangle those knots and smooth out the frayed edges of my mental state. Exercise offers profound physiological and psychological benefits that can elevate mood and alleviate anxiety. When you engage in physical activity, your body releases endorphins. These "feel-good" hormones act as natural painkillers and mood elevators. They create a euphoria and well-being, often called the "runner's high." Simultaneously, exercise reduces levels of stress hormones like cortisol, which can wreak havoc on your mental health when elevated. This dual action does exercise a powerful ally in managing symptoms of anxiety and depression.

Exercise also plays a critical role in enhancing the outcomes of Cognitive Behavioral Therapy (CBT). Regular physical activity can significantly improve focus and concentration, making it easier to engage with CBT practices. When your mind is sharp and attentive, you're better equipped to explore and challenge the thought patterns that contribute to anxiety and depression. Additionally, exercise promotes mood stability, providing a steady emotional baseline that supports stress management. Incorporating exercise into your routine creates a supportive environment for CBT, amplifying its effectiveness and fostering a more resilient mindset. The synergy between physical activity and CBT can empower you to navigate life's challenges with greater ease and confidence.

To support mental well-being, consider integrating specific exercises into your routine. Aerobic activities like running, swimming, and cycling are effective in boosting mood and reducing anxiety. These exercises increase heart rate and circulation, promoting cardiovascular health while releasing endorphins. Engaging in aerobic exercise for at least 30 minutes a few times a week can profoundly impact your mental health. Mind-body exercises such as yoga and tai chi offer additional benefits, combining physical movement with mindfulness and breath control. These practices promote relaxation and mental clarity, helping you connect with your body and calm your mind. Regular exercise can be a cornerstone of your mental health strategy, whether a brisk walk or a gentle yoga session.

Consider the story of Alex, who found solace in running to manage depressive symptoms. Initially resistant to exercise, Alex started with short jogs around the neighborhood. Over time, these runs became a source of joy and empowerment, lifting Alex's mood and providing clarity. The rhythmic movement of running allowed Alex to process thoughts and emotions, creating a meditative space that complemented CBT techniques. Similarly, Rachel discovered the benefits of combining yoga with CBT to reduce anxiety. The gentle stretches and mindful breathing in yoga helped Rachel release physical tension and cultivate peace. This practice allowed Rachel to approach CBT sessions with a calm and open mind, enhancing the effectiveness of therapeutic interventions.

These stories illustrate the transformative potential of exercise in managing anxiety and depression. By incorporating regular physical activity into your life, you can tap into a powerful resource that supports mental health and complements CBT practices. Exercise is not just about physical fitness; it's about nurturing your mind and body, creating a foundation for resilience and well-being. Whether lacing up your running shoes or unrolling a yoga mat, each step, each breath, is a step towards healing and empowerment.

5.3 SPIRITUALITY, FAITH, AND CBT: A HARMONIOUS APPROACH

Spirituality can be a profound anchor in times of emotional turmoil, offering a sense of purpose and meaning that transcends our immediate challenges. It's not about subscribing to a particular religion or doctrine but about connecting with something greater than ourselves, whether it be a sense of higher consciousness, nature, or community. This connection can provide comfort and guidance, helping us navigate the complexities of life with a broader perspective. For those grappling with anxiety and depression, spirituality can offer a sanctuary of peace and acceptance, reminding us that we are part of a larger tapestry where each thread, including our own, holds significance and worth.

Integrating spirituality with Cognitive Behavioral Therapy (CBT) creates a unique harmony that can enhance emotional well-being. Spiritual reflections can play a vital role in cognitive restructuring, a core component of CBT. By reflecting on spiritual teachings or personal beliefs, you can challenge and reframe negative thoughts in a way that aligns with your values and aspirations. This approach not only supports the cognitive processes involved in CBT, but also deepens your connection to your spiritual path, providing a holistic framework for healing. This integration can transform the therapeutic process into a more meaningful and fulfilling experience, as it honors the mind and the spirit.

Several spiritual practices align naturally with CBT, offering complementary activities that support mental health. Meditation and prayer are powerful tools for stress reduction, providing moments of stillness and introspection. Through meditation, you can cultivate a state of inner calm and awareness, allowing you to observe your thoughts without judgment. Whether through traditional religious practices or personal affirmations, prayer can be a source of strength and solace, offering a channel for expressing hopes, fears, and gratitude. Mindful contemplation and reflection invite you to explore your beliefs and values, encouraging a deeper understanding of yourself and your place in the world. These practices can enhance the effectiveness of CBT by fostering a sense of connection and purpose, reinforcing the therapeutic work you are doing.

Consider the story of Anna, who found strength in her faith while navigating therapy. Struggling with depression, Anna turned to spiritual teachings as a source of guidance and hope. By integrating these reflections into her CBT sessions, she could reframe her negative thoughts in a way that resonated with her spiritual beliefs. This process enriched her therapy and deepened her faith, creating a harmonious balance between the two. Similarly, many individuals benefit from attending spiritual retreats as part of their holistic CBT approach. These retreats offer a dedicated space for reflection and renewal, allowing participants to immerse themselves in spiritual practices that complement their therapeutic journey. The combination of structured CBT work and spiritual exploration can lead to profound insights and healing, as it addresses well-being's psychological and spiritual dimensions.

The relationship between spirituality and mental health is profoundly personal, and the integration of spiritual practices with CBT can be customized to align with your unique beliefs and experiences. Whether it's through meditation, prayer, or reflection, spirituality offers a rich resource for emotional resilience and healing. By weaving these practices into your CBT work, you create a tapestry of support that honors all aspects of your being. This holistic approach enhances your mental health and nurtures your spirit, providing peace and purpose amid life's challenges.

5.4 CREATING A PERSONAL WELLNESS TOOLKIT

Think of a personal wellness toolkit as your mental health first aid kit, filled with strategies and practices tailored to your unique needs. It's a collection of tools designed to support your mental well-being, much like a physical toolkit would help you fix things around the house. The components of a wellness toolkit are varied, reflecting the diverse aspects of life that impact your mental health. From Cognitive Behavioral Therapy (CBT) techniques to exercise routines and nutritional plans, each element plays a role in maintaining balance and resilience. This toolkit isn't a one-size-fits-all solution. Instead, it's personalized to fit you, acknowledging that what works for one person might not be as effective for another. Personalization is critical in mental health practices because it recognizes that each individual's experiences, preferences, and challenges are distinct. Tailoring strategies to fit your needs ensures that your chosen tools are practical, sustainable, and enjoyable. This approach empowers you to take charge of your mental health in a way that feels authentic and aligned with who you are.

Building a comprehensive wellness toolkit involves exploring strategies and selecting those that resonate with you. Start by considering the different facets of your life that impact your mental health. Journaling is therapeutic, offering a space to express and process your thoughts. Incorporating CBT techniques can provide structure and support in challenging negative thought patterns. Whether it's a daily walk or a weekly yoga class, exercise routines can enhance your physical and emotional well-being. Nutritional plans focusing on whole foods can nourish your body and mind, supporting overall health. By blending these elements, you create a toolkit that's as unique as you are, reflecting your needs and goals.

Consider Jane, who crafted her wellness toolkit by combining journaling, yoga, and healthy eating. Each morning, she begins with a gentle yoga session, grounding herself and setting a positive tone for the day. She takes moments to jot down her thoughts and feelings throughout the day, using journaling to reflect and release. Her meals are thoughtfully planned and rich in nutrients that support her mental clarity and energy. This combination of practices creates a balanced approach to her mental health, providing her with the tools she needs to navigate life's challenges with grace and resilience. Jane's toolkit is not static; it evolves as her life changes, adapting to new circumstances and challenges.

Adapting your wellness toolkit to fit changing life circumstances is crucial for maintaining effectiveness. Life is dynamic, and so should be your approach to mental health. Your needs may shift as you transition through different stages, whether starting a new job, moving to a new city, or experiencing a personal loss. Your toolkit should reflect these changes, incorporating new strategies or modifying existing ones to support you better. This adaptability ensures that your toolkit remains relevant and valuable, providing the foundation to thrive amidst change. Regularly assessing and adjusting your toolkit aligns it with your current reality, ensuring that it continues serving you effectively.

In weaving these practices into your life, you build a personalized wellness toolkit that supports your mental health journey. Each tool and each practice is a step toward greater resilience and well-being. This toolkit empowers you to face life's challenges confidently, knowing that you have a set of strategies tailored to your unique needs. As you explore and refine your toolkit, you deepen your understanding of yourself and your mental health, creating a foundation for lasting change and growth. With your toolkit, you are equipped to navigate the complexities of life, embracing each moment with clarity and strength.

MAKE A DIFFERENCE WITH YOUR REVIEW

UNLOCK THE POWER OF GENEROSITY

"The best way to find yourself is to lose yourself in the service of others."

— MAHATMA GANDHI

People who give without expecting anything in return lead fuller, happier lives. Together, we can make a difference.

Would you help someone like yourself—someone seeking relief from anxiety or depression and eager to begin a journey toward peace and well-being?

My mission is to make the life-changing methods of Cognitive Behavioral Therapy (CBT) approachable and accessible for anyone who needs it.

But to reach more people, I need your help.

Most readers choose books based on reviews. By sharing your experience with this book, you're helping another person take that first step towards a happier, more resilient mindset. It costs nothing and takes less than a minute but could change someone's mental health journey. Your review could help one more person find inner calm and hope...one more individual manage their challenges with clarity. ...one more reader start their own path to healing and self-compassion.

Scan the QR code to leave a review.

If you love helping others, you're my kind of person. Thank you from the bottom of my heart!

— **Dotty Lynn**

6

PERSONALIZED CBT APPROACHES

When I began exploring Cognitive Behavioral Therapy (CBT), it felt like standing beneath a mountain, unsure where to start the climb. The path seemed daunting, with its twists and turns obscured by uncertainty. It wasn't until I realized the power of a personalized approach that the fog began to lift. Crafting a plan tailored to my unique experiences and challenges transformed CBT from an overwhelming prospect into an empowering journey. Like a skilled guide, a personalized CBT plan helps you navigate your mental landscape with precision and purpose, focusing on your individual needs and strengths.

The first step in crafting your personalized CBT plan involves a deep dive into self-assessment. Understanding your specific challenges and goals is crucial for creating a focused strategy. Self-assessment questionnaires can be invaluable, helping you identify the particular issues you face. These questionnaires guide you through introspective questions about your thoughts, feelings, and behaviors, revealing patterns and areas that need attention. Once you've identified your primary concerns, it's time to set **SMART goals—Specific, Measurable, Achievable, Relevant, and Time-bound goals**. These goals provide clarity and direction, ensuring your CBT plan is grounded and tailored to your unique journey. By articulating what you want to achieve, you create a roadmap for your therapeutic process, making tracking progress and celebrating milestones easier.

Personal CBT Self-Assessment Questionnaire:

1. **Identify Negative Thoughts:**
   - What specific negative thoughts do you often experience in stressful situations?
     - (Example: I can't get anything right.")
2. **Frequency of thoughts:**
   - How often do you notice these negative thoughts during the week?
     - (Rate on a scale of 1-5, where 1 = Rarely and 5 = Very Often)
3. **Cognitive distortions:**
   - Do you recognize any patterns of cognitive distortions in your thinking?
     - (Example: All-or-Nothing Thinking, Overgeneralization, Catastrophizing) which
     - ones apply?
4. **Challenging Thoughts:**
   - Do you recognize any patterns of cognitive distortions in your thinking?
     - (Write down at least two pieces of evidence.)

5. **Emotional triggers:**
   - What situations tend to trigger strong emotional responses for you?
     - (List a few situations or events.)
6. **Intensity of feelings:**
   - When you experience negative emotions (e.g., sadness, anger, anxiety), how tense are they typically?
     - (Rate on a scale of 1-10)
7. **Physical reactions:**
   - How does your body react when you experience these feelings?
     - (Examples: Tension, Fatigue, Rapid Heartbeat)
8. **Positive emotions:**
   - What activities or interactions make you feel optimistic?
     - (List a few examples that uplift your mood.)
9. **Behavioral Patterns:**
   - What behaviors do you engage in when you experience negative thoughts or feelings?
     - (Examples: Avoidance, Aggression, Withdrawing)
10. **Coping strategies:**
    - What strategies do you currently use to cope with stress or negative emotions?
      - (Evaluate their effectiveness: 1 = Not Effective, 5 = Very Effective)
11. **Behavioral consequences:**
    - How do your behaviors influence your overall well-being or relationships?
      - (Reflect on both positive and negative impacts.)

12. **Desired changes:**
    ◦ What changes would you like to make regarding your thoughts, feelings, or behaviors?
      ▪ (Realistic goals for improvement.)

Reflection:

1. **Pattern Recognition:**
   ◦ After considering your answers, what patterns do you notice in your thoughts, feelings, and behaviors?
2. **Areas of attention:**
   ◦ Which areas stand out as needing the most attention or change?
     ▪ (Prioritize based on your reflections)
3. **Next steps:**
   ◦ What practical steps can you take to address these areas?
     ▪ (Consider small, manageable actions you can implement.)

Take time to reflect on your responses and consider discussing them with a therapist or trusted friend if possible. This process can help you gain insight into your patterns and foster personal growth.

Setting **SMART (Specific, Measurable, Achievable, Relevant, and Time-Bound)** goals for cognitive behavioral therapy can help you make meaningful changes in your thoughts, emotions, and behaviors. Here's how you can structure these goals using the smart criteria:

1. **Specific:**
    - **Goal:** Instead of saying, "I want to feel better," specify what that means to you.
    - **Example:** "I hope to reduce my anxiety about social situations."
2. **Measurable:**
    - **Goal:** Define how you will measure progress.
    - **Example:** "I will track my anxiety levels on a scale of 1-10 before and after social events."
3. **Achievable:**
    - **Goal:** Ensure that your goal is realistic, given your current situation and resources.
    - **Example:** "I will practice attending one social event per week for the next month."
4. **Relevant:**
    - **Goal:** Make sure the goal aligns with your overall therapy objectives and personal values.
    - **Example:** Reducing my anxiety and social situations will help me strengthen my relationships and quality of life."
5. **Time-Bound:**
    - **Goal:** Set a deadline for achieving your goal.
    - **Example:** "I will achieve this by the end of the next 4 weeks."

Additional SMART Goals for CBT:

- **Cognitive restructuring goal:**
    - **Specific:** "I want to identify and challenge my negative thoughts."
    - **Measurable:** "I will write down at least three negative thoughts each day."

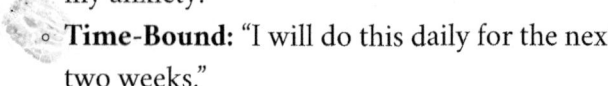

- ◦ **Achievable:** "I will use a thought record sheet."
  - ◦ **Relevant:** "This will help me gain control over my anxiety."
  - ◦ **Time-Bound:** "I will do this daily for the next two weeks."
- **Behavioral activation goal:**
  - ◦ **Specific:** "I want to engage in pleasurable activities more often."
  - ◦ **Measurable:** "I will schedule at least three enjoyable activities each week."
  - ◦ **Achievable:** "I'll choose activities that are easy for me to do."
  - ◦ **Relevant:** "This will help improve my mood and decrease feelings of sadness."
  - ◦ **Time bound:** "I will maintain this schedule for the next month."
- **Mindfulness goal:**
  - ◦ **Specific:** "I want to incorporate mindfulness into my daily routine."
  - ◦ **Measurable:** "I will practice mindfulness for 10 minutes each morning."
  - ◦ **Achievable:** "I'll use a mindfulness app to guide me."
  - ◦ **Relevant:** "This will help reduce my overall stress levels."
  - ◦ **Time-Bound:** "I will do this every day for the next two weeks."

With your goals in place, the next step is to outline a strategy that aligns with your personal preferences and priorities. CBT offers many techniques, from cognitive restructuring to exposure therapy, and selecting those that resonate with you is vital. Consider your comfort level and readiness for each method and prioritize areas that require focused work. For example, suppose social anxiety is a significant concern. In that case, you might choose techniques like role-playing or gradual exposure to social situations, allowing you to build confidence and resilience over time. By tailoring your approach, you ensure your CBT plan is effective and sustainable, fitting seamlessly into your lifestyle.

Flexibility is vital when it comes to a personalized CBT plan. Just as life is dynamic, so should your therapy approach be adaptable. Regularly review and adjust your plan based on your progress and evolving needs. This adaptability allows you to refine your strategies, incorporating new insights and experiences as you move forward. Like a gardener tending to their plants, nurturing your CBT plan with flexibility ensures that it continues to grow and thrive, supporting your mental health journey.

To illustrate the power of personalized CBT, consider the story of Emily, who faced debilitating social anxiety. Her initial plan focused on small, manageable steps, like making eye contact or initiating brief conversations. As her confidence grew, she adapted her plan to include more challenging goals, such as attending social gatherings or speaking up in meetings. This gradual progression allowed her to build resilience and overcome her fears. Meanwhile, Jake's work-related stress was managed through a different approach. He prioritized techniques like cognitive restructuring and mindfulness, focusing on changing his perception of workplace stressors. Jake managed his stress effectively by regularly revisiting and adjusting his plan, enhancing his professional and personal life.

Reflection Section: Craft Your Plan

Take a moment to reflect on your unique challenges and goals. Use a self-assessment questionnaire to identify specific issues. Please write down your SMART goals, ensuring they are clear and achievable. Consider which CBT techniques align with your preferences and priorities. Regularly review and adapt your plan, noting any progress or areas for improvement. This exercise will help you create a personalized CBT plan that empowers you to navigate your mental health journey confidently and clearly.

6.1 ADAPTING CBT TECHNIQUES FOR DIFFERENT SITUATIONS

Life often throws us into diverse scenarios, each with its challenges. In these moments, Cognitive Behavioral Therapy (CBT) becomes a flexible ally, offering techniques that can be tailored to suit various contexts. This situational adaptation of CBT is crucial because all situations are different. What works in one setting might need a slight tweak in another. Understanding the dynamic nature of CBT means recognizing that its applications are as varied as the challenges we face. It requires a willingness to modify techniques, ensuring they address the specific demands of each context you encounter.

Consider the workplace, where stress can sometimes pile up like an avalanche. Adapting thought records—a CBT tool that helps track and challenge negative thinking—can be particularly beneficial in such environments. You might be overwhelmed by a looming deadline, thinking, "I'll never finish on time." Using a thought record, you can dissect this belief, identify cognitive distortions like catastrophizing, and replace them with more balanced thoughts. Perhaps, "I've met tight deadlines before, and I can do it again by prioritizing tasks." This adaptation turns a generic CBT technique into a personalized strategy for managing workplace stress.

Public speaking anxiety presents another challenge where situational adaptation is critical. Exposure therapy, a staple in CBT, involves gradually facing fears to reduce anxiety. In this case, you might start by practicing your speech alone, in front of a mirror, and eventually with a small group of supportive friends. Each step builds confidence, reducing the fear of judgment. Modifying exposure therapy in this way allows you to face your anxiety incrementally, transforming it from a daunting obstacle into a manageable task.

Environmental factors play a significant role in how we experience and manage anxiety. Crowded environments, for instance, can be overwhelming, triggering feelings of panic or claustrophobia. Here, situational adaptation involves using techniques like grounding exercises to stay present. By focusing on physical sensations—such as feeling your feet on the ground or the texture of an object in your hand—you anchor yourself at that moment, reducing anxiety's grip. This adaptability allows you to handle crowded places with greater ease, turning potentially stressful situations into opportunities for practicing resilience.

Real-life adaptations of CBT techniques illustrate their versatility. Take the example of someone dealing with travel-related anxiety. Airports and flights can be anxiety-inducing, with their bustling crowds and confined spaces. By adapting

CBT, they might use visualization techniques to imagine a calm, peaceful place while waiting at the gate. This mental escape provides comfort amidst the chaos, helping them manage their anxiety. Similarly, home-based challenges, like navigating family dynamics, require tailored approaches. For instance, adapting CBT to improve communication skills within the family can help reduce misunderstandings and foster a supportive environment.

These examples highlight the importance of viewing CBT as a toolkit, ready to be adapted to whatever life throws your way. By understanding the dynamic nature of its applications, you can modify techniques to fit the unique contexts and challenges you face. This adaptability enhances the effectiveness of CBT and empowers you to approach each situation with confidence and creativity.

6.2 ADDRESSING UNIQUE COGNITIVE DISTORTIONS

Cognitive distortions are like funhouse mirrors, warping reality in ways that can intensify feelings of anxiety and depression. While many are familiar with common distortions like all-or-nothing thinking or overgeneralization, other, less apparent distortions can be particularly tricky to recognize and address. Take magical thinking, for instance. This distortion involves believing that your thoughts, feelings, or actions can influence unrelated events. You might think, "If I wear my lucky socks, the meeting will go well," when it doesn't, you're left feeling anxious or disappointed. Emotional reasoning is another subtle distortion, where you assume that how you feel reflects the truth. If you're feeling inadequate, you might conclude, "I am inadequate," even when evidence suggests otherwise. Recognizing these unique distortions requires a keen eye and a willingness to question the narrative they create.

Identifying the unique cognitive distortions can make journaling an invaluable tool. By documenting specific instances of distorted thinking, you create a space to reflect and analyze your thoughts. For example, you might write about a time when magical thinking led you to avoid a situation out of fear of a negative outcome. As you review your entries, patterns may emerge, revealing how these distortions influence your emotions and behaviors. This process of reflection can illuminate the hidden scripts that govern your thoughts, making them easier to challenge and change. It's a bit like detective work, piecing together clues to uncover the underlying assumptions driving your anxiety or depression.

Once you've identified these distortions, developing personalized thought-challenging questions is next. These questions challenge the narrative created by your distortions, encouraging you to consider alternative perspectives. For magical thinking, you might ask yourself, "Is there a real connection between my thoughts and these events, or am I attributing power to coincidence?" For emotional reasoning, questions like, "What evidence supports this feeling as fact?" can help separate emotions from reality. Practicing mindfulness can further aid in detaching from these distorted thoughts. Observing your thoughts without judgment creates space between yourself and the distortion, allowing you to respond intentionally rather than impulsively.

Consider the case of someone grappling with magical thinking in the context of relationship anxiety. One might believe that thinking about a breakup will cause it to happen. By recognizing this distortion, individuals can challenge it with evidence-based questions, gradually reducing its hold on them. Exercises for emotional reasoning in professional settings involve role-playing scenarios where you practice distinguishing between feelings and facts. For instance, if you feel overlooked in a meeting, instead of concluding, "I'm invisible," you might consider alternative explanations, such as the dynamics of the discussion or the focus on other topics. These exercises empower you to approach situations with a clearer, more balanced perspective, reducing the emotional charge of cognitive distortions.

Addressing unique cognitive distortions is like peeling away layers of an onion, revealing the core beliefs that shape your experiences. As you work through these layers, you likely find the world less daunting and your mind more at ease. By tackling these distortions head-on, you open the door to improved mental health and greater control over your thoughts and emotions.

6.3 OVERCOMING CBT CHALLENGES: STAYING MOTIVATED

Embarking on the path of Cognitive Behavioral Therapy (CBT) often feels refreshing at the start, much like setting out on a new adventure with fresh energy. However, maintaining motivation can become a struggle as the initial excitement wanes. A common hurdle many face is the need for immediate results. You might think, "Why am I not feeling better yet?" it can lead to frustration, causing doubt about the effectiveness of the techniques. It's important to remember that CBT is a process that requires patience and persistence. The changes you seek might not immediately be evident, but each small step contributes to progress. Another challenge is establishing a consistent practice. Life's demands can easily disrupt your routine, making it challenging to keep up with therapy exercises. Without regular practice, it's easy to feel like you're losing ground, which can further diminish motivation.

To stay engaged with CBT long-term, consider implementing strategies that boost motivation and commitment. One practical approach is setting short-term rewards for achieving your goals. These rewards can be as simple as treating yourself to a favorite activity or enjoying a special meal. Small incentives can make the process more enjoyable, providing motivating milestones. Visual progress trackers are another tool that can help. By charting your improvements, you create a tangible record of your journey, allowing you to see how far you've come. These visual reminders can be incredibly encouraging, offering a sense of accomplishment even when progress feels slow. Remember, motivation is not a constant; it ebbs and flows. Finding ways to celebrate small wins can make a big difference in maintaining momentum.

There will inevitably be times when your interest in CBT wanes, and you might feel like you're hitting a plateau. During these periods of stagnation, it's essential to reignite your commitment. Joining a CBT support group can provide accountability and a sense of community. Sharing experiences with others on a similar path can offer fresh perspectives and encouragement. You're not alone in facing challenges; hearing how others navigate them can be inspiring. Rotating techniques can also prevent monotony. If one approach feels stale, try integrating another. This variation can bring a new spark to your practice, keeping it dynamic and engaging. Remember, flexibility is vital. Adjusting your approach can keep your practice alive and responsive to your needs.

Consider the story of Tom, who initially struggled with his CBT routine after a setback. Feeling disheartened, he reached out to a support group, where he found camaraderie and reassurance. Listening to others' stories reminded him of his progress, sparking a renewed interest in his practice. He began experimenting with different techniques, eventually creating a routine aligned more with his current needs. Similarly, Jessica found herself losing steam midway through her CBT journey. She regained her enthusiasm by introducing visual trackers and setting small rewards for herself. Seeing her achievements laid out visually helped her appreciate the progress she was making, even when it felt slow. These examples highlight the importance of adaptability and community in sustaining motivation.

6.4 TAILORING CBT TO YOUR LIFESTYLE

Incorporating Cognitive Behavioral Therapy (CBT) into your daily life can transform it from a structured therapy session into a seamless part of your routine. Think of it as weaving CBT into the fabric of your day, creating natural points for practice that feel intuitive rather than forced. Start by identifying those moments in your day when you can naturally introduce CBT techniques. Perhaps it's during your morning coffee when you're already in a reflective state. This is an ideal moment to practice mindfulness by focusing entirely on the aroma and warmth of your drink and grounding yourself in the present. These small pockets of time are opportunities to engage with CBT without setting aside additional blocks of your day.

Aligning CBT with personal habits doesn't mean over-hauling your entire routine. Instead, it's about integrating techniques that complement what you're already doing. For example, consider incorporating mindfulness into your morning rituals. As you brush your teeth or shower, focus on the sensations—the sound of water and the feel of the tooth-brush. This simple practice can anchor your mind, setting a calm and focused tone for the day ahead.

Similarly, using CBT techniques during your daily commute can transform a mundane or stressful experience into personal growth. Whether driving, cycling, or taking public transport, use this time to engage in deep breathing exercises or listen to a CBT-guided meditation. These practices can help regulate your mood, making your commute a time of relaxation rather than stress.

The benefits of aligning CBT with your lifestyle are manifold. Integrating these practices naturally reduces the barriers to regular engagement, making it easier to maintain consistency. This approach ensures that CBT becomes a part of your life rather than an addition. Consistency enhances effectiveness; the more regularly you practice, the more ingrained these techniques become. They start to feel like second nature, a default way of responding to the world around them. This natural incorporation not only enhances your ability to manage anxiety and depression but also fosters a greater sense of control and empowerment over your mental health.

Consider the experience of a busy professional who effectively aligned CBT with work breaks. Instead of scrolling through emails or social media, they used these breaks to engage in quick mindfulness exercises, such as focusing on their breath or observing their surroundings with a beginner's mind. This practice provided moments of calm amidst a hectic day, reducing stress and enhancing focus. Another example is of someone tailoring CBT exercises for family-oriented routines. They incorporated gratitude journaling into their family meals, where each member would share something positive from their day. This practice reinforced CBT principles, strengthened family bonds, and fostered a positive atmosphere at home.

These narratives illustrate how CBT can be woven into the various threads of daily life, enhancing individual mental health and the quality of interactions with others. As you explore these strategies, remember that finding what works best for you is a personal journey. The goal is to create a

CBT practice that feels as natural as breathing, seamlessly supporting your mental well-being.

Blending CBT with everyday life lays the groundwork for a more balanced and resilient mindset. As you continue to explore these techniques, you'll discover new ways to integrate them into your routine, reinforcing the skills and insights you've gained. This approach not only strengthens your ability to manage anxiety and depression but also enriches your overall experience, making everyday moments opportunities for growth and healing.

7

REAL-WORLD APPLICATIONS AND CASE STUDIES

W e all know the feeling of standing before a crowd, heart pounding, sweaty palms, and the mind racing with thoughts of inadequacy. For a young professional named Alex, this was an everyday reality. Speaking anxiety had gripped him tightly, making every presentation at work feel like an insurmountable hurdle. But Alex's journey through

Cognitive Behavioral Therapy (CBT) transformed this narrative. Through exposure therapy, he slowly exposed himself to speaking situations in a controlled manner. Starting with small group meetings and gradually working up to more extensive presentations, Alex faced his fears head-on. This method of gradual desensitization helped him chip away at the anxiety that once dictated his professional life.

Alex also engaged in cognitive restructuring to challenge the negative beliefs that fueled his anxiety. He learned to question the automatic thoughts that told him, "I'll embarrass myself," and "Everyone will judge me." By replacing these with more balanced thoughts like, "I've prepared well, and I can handle this," Alex discovered a new sense of confidence. This shift didn't happen overnight, but perseverance made it a cornerstone of his personal growth. As Alex's confidence grew, so did his self-efficacy, enabling him to navigate social situations with newfound ease and assurance. The emotional impact of his success extended beyond the office, enriching his interactions and bolstering his resilience.

Consider another story—this one of Sarah, who faced a different kind of anxiety. For Sarah, travel was a source of both excitement and dread. The thought of navigating airports, encountering crowds, and interacting with strangers triggered intense social anxiety. Yet, with the help of CBT, Sarah embarked on a journey of personal transformation. Exposure therapy played a crucial role here as well. By gradually exposing herself to travel-related situations, Sarah learned to manage her anxiety. She began with short trips to familiar places, focusing on the sensations of travel without letting fear take the reins. This practice allowed her to build resilience, slowly extending her comfort zone with each experience.

Cognitive restructuring helped Sarah address her fear of judgment during travel. She realized that the thought, "Everyone is watching and judging me," reflected her insecurities more than reality. By challenging this belief, she could engage with her surroundings without the weight of imagined scrutiny. Through these techniques, Sarah achieved a greater sense of emotional resilience. Her confidence in social settings grew, and travel transformed from a source of anxiety to an opportunity for adventure and growth. This newfound empowerment was a testament to the power of CBT in reshaping one's experience of the world.

Quotes from those who have triumphed over anxiety offer insight into their journeys. Alex shares, "CBT taught me that facing my fears was like training a muscle—the more I did it, the stronger I became." His reflection captures the essence of gradual exposure, highlighting the cumulative power of small, consistent efforts. Meanwhile, Sarah reflects, "Every step I took outside my comfort zone brought me closer to the life I wanted, not the one my anxiety dictated." Her words remind us of the value of perseverance and the profound change that can come from challenging our fears.

These stories illustrate the transformative power of CBT, showcasing how individuals can move from anxiety to empowerment. Exposure therapy techniques and cognitive restructuring provide a framework for personal growth, enabling you to face fears with courage and resilience. The emotional and personal growth achieved through CBT extends beyond the absence of anxiety; it is about embracing life fully and authentically. As you read these stories, let them inspire you to explore how CBT might offer the tools you need to navigate your challenges.

7.1 CASE STUDY: CBT IN ACTION FOR WORKPLACE ANXIETY

Meet Emily, a talented graphic designer working in a high-pressure advertising firm. Her creativity was unmatched, but anxiety loomed like a shadow over her career. Her job's fast-paced nature, tight deadlines, and constant client meetings pushed her to the brink. Emily often felt overwhelmed, leading to sleepless nights and continuous dread as she navigated her professional world. Her anxiety manifested in physical symptoms, such as headaches and fatigue, which further hindered her performance. The cycle was vicious: stress led to anxiety, which led to poor performance, and the resulting self-doubt fed back into her anxiety. Seeking relief, Emily turned to Cognitive Behavioral Therapy (CBT) to reclaim her sense of work-life balance and well-being.

Emily's CBT plan was tailored specifically to address her workplace anxiety. The approach began with time management techniques to help her navigate the demanding environment. By breaking her workload into smaller, manageable tasks, Emily could tackle one piece at a time, reducing the overwhelming nature of her responsibilities. This strategy alleviated immediate stress and helped her focus, improving her productivity. Cognitive restructuring was another vital component, allowing Emily to challenge the negative beliefs that fueled her anxiety. She learned to question thoughts like, "I'll never meet this deadline," and replace them with more constructive ones, such as, "I can create a plan and tackle this project step by step." This shift in mindset was instrumental in reducing her anxiety levels.

Mindfulness played a significant role in Emily's journey as well. By incorporating mindfulness practices into her daily routine, Emily found a way to anchor herself amidst the chaos. Simple exercises, like mindful breathing and body scans, became part of her breaks, offering moments of tranquility that countered the stress of her workday. These practices helped her remain present and focused, reducing the likelihood of getting swept up in anxious thoughts. Through

CBT, Emily discovered that she could cultivate a sense of calm and control, even in a high-pressure environment.

The outcomes of Emily's CBT intervention were profound. Her anxiety levels decreased significantly, and she experienced a marked improvement in her job performance. With the tools to manage her stress, Emily could approach her work with renewed confidence and clarity. This transformation extended to her communication and interpersonal skills. By challenging her negative self-talk, Emily found that she could express herself more assertively in meetings and collaborate more effectively with her colleagues. Her enhanced communication skills fostered better relationships at work, creating a supportive network that alleviated her anxiety.

Reflecting on her experience, Emily realized the importance of consistency in CBT practice. The techniques she learned were not one-time fixes but habits that required ongoing commitment. Emily maintained her progress by integrating CBT into her daily work routine. She scheduled regular mindfulness breaks and continued to set realistic goals, ensuring that the tools she had learned remained a part of her life. Emily's journey illustrates how tailored CBT strategies can be applied to manage workplace anxiety effectively, offering a roadmap for others facing similar challenges.

For those navigating workplace stress, Emily's experience offers valuable insights. Consistency in practice is vital; the more you integrate these techniques into your routine, the more natural they become. Taking time to understand and challenge your thoughts can lead to meaningful change. Whether through setting realistic goals, practicing mindfulness, or restructuring thoughts, the tailored application of CBT can transform workplace anxiety into an opportunity for growth and resilience.

7.2 PERSONAL NARRATIVES: TRANSFORMING DEPRESSION

Imagine the weight of academic pressure pressing down on you like a heavy cloud, obscuring any sense of achievement or self-worth. This is where we find Jason, a college student who once thrived on the excitement of learning but found himself trapped in a cycle of despair. Depression had crept in, turning once manageable tasks into insurmountable obstacles. Jason's story is one of resilience and transformation through Cognitive Behavioral Therapy. The technique of behavioral activation was pivotal in his recovery. By incrementally increasing his engagement with activities he once loved, Jason reignited his passion for study and life. This method involved setting small, achievable goals—like attending one class or studying for an hour—gradually building up his confidence and motivation. This shift, though gradual, allowed Jason to reclaim his sense of purpose and joy in learning.

In another corner of life, we meet Maria, a new mother grappling with the shadows of postpartum depression. The joy of welcoming a new life was overshadowed by feelings of inadequacy and overwhelming sadness. For Maria, the path to healing began with CBT's cognitive restructuring. She learned to identify and challenge the negative thought patterns that told her she was failing as a parent. By reframing these thoughts, Maria found the strength to embrace her role with grace and compassion. She replaced thoughts like, "I'm not a good mother," with affirmations of her efforts and love. This change in mindset was instrumental in her emotional recovery, allowing her to nurture her child from a place of self-acceptance rather than self-doubt.

Through CBT, Jason and Maria experienced significant changes in their emotional and lifestyle habits. For Jason, the fog of depression began to lift as he engaged more fully in his studies and social life. His emotional stability improved, and he developed a resilience to face academic challenges with a clearer mind and a more optimistic outlook. On the other hand, Maria found that her newfound perspective brought a sense of balance and peace to her daily life. She developed healthier routines, incorporating self-care practices that nurtured her well-being alongside her responsibilities as a mother. These changes were not just surface-level adjustments, but deep-seated transformations that improved their overall quality of life.

Reflecting on their journeys, both Jason and Maria emphasize the importance of persistence. Jason admits there were days when motivation was scarce, and the temptation to give in to despair was strong. Yet, he found that he could gradually build momentum toward recovery by sticking to his CBT practices, even in small ways. Maria echoes this sentiment, highlighting the value of seeking support from loved ones and professionals. She stresses that reaching out for help was a crucial step in her healing process, providing the encouragement and guidance needed to navigate the complexities of postpartum depression.

For those facing similar challenges, Jason and Maria offer words of encouragement: "Be patient with yourself," Jason advises, "and celebrate every small victory because they add up to significant changes." Maria adds, "Don't be afraid to ask for help. You're not alone, and there's strength in seeking support." Their stories remind us that depression, while daunting, does not have to define your life. With the right tools and support, transformation is possible.

7.3 SUCCESS STORIES: INTEGRATING CBT AND SPIRITUAL BELIEFS

In the serene quiet of her meditation space, Emily sits with her eyes closed, her mind focusing on her breath, each inhale and exhale a step toward tranquility. For years, anxiety had been a constant presence in Emily's life, a shadow that seemed to follow her everywhere. Seeking relief, she turned to Cognitive Behavioral Therapy (CBT). She discovered a new path when she began integrating meditation into her practice. This fusion of CBT and meditation became her anchor, allowing her to explore the depths of her thoughts while finding peace in the present moment. Emily found that the reflective nature of meditation complemented the analytical approach of CBT, enabling her to challenge negative thought patterns with greater clarity and calm. Through this harmonious blend, she experienced a profound reduction in anxiety, feeling more grounded and centered than she had in years.

In another part of the world, David found solace in prayer as he navigated his mental health journey. Raised in a spiritual household, David had always turned to prayer during times of distress. He felt relieved when he began CBT. Initially, he was uncertain about how his spiritual beliefs would integrate with the structured framework of therapy. However, he soon realized that prayer could be a powerful tool in supporting his CBT practice. By incorporating prayer into his daily routine, David found that he could reflect on his thoughts with compassion and understanding. His spiritual reflections supported thought restructuring, helping him replace negative thoughts with ones grounded in faith and hope. David's journey illustrates how spiritual practices can enhance CBT, providing strength and resilience through faith.

Integrating spirituality and CBT led to significant emotional and spiritual growth for Emily and David. For Emily, meditation not only reduced her anxiety but also increased her sense of peace and purpose. She found that the quiet moments spent in meditation deepened her connection to herself and the world around her. This spiritual fulfillment enhanced her emotional resilience, allowing her to face challenges with newfound grace and composure. Similarly, David's incorporating prayer into his CBT practice gave him a sense of spiritual fulfillment that enriched his emotional well-being. The strength he found in his faith bolstered his resilience, empowering him to navigate his mental health journey with courage and confidence.

Emily and David offer valuable insights to those considering integrating spirituality with CBT. Emily suggested using simple meditation practices, such as mindful breathing or body scans, to complement CBT techniques. These practices can be easily incorporated into your daily routine, providing a foundation for deeper reflection and growth. David encourages exploring personal beliefs in therapy and using spiritual reflections to support cognitive restructuring. He highlights the importance of finding spiritual practices that resonate with you through prayer, meditation, or other reflective activities. By blending these practices with CBT, you can create a holistic approach that honors your mental and spiritual well-being.

As you explore the integration of spirituality and CBT, remember that this process is deeply personal. What works for one person may not work for another, so it's important to find practices that align with your beliefs and values. By embracing this integration, you open the door to a richer, more fulfilling experience of therapy, one that nurtures both your mind and spirit. This harmonious blend offers a path to mental health and a journey toward a more balanced and authentic life.

7.4 LESSONS LEARNED: OVERCOMING THERAPY FRUSTRATIONS

Many people approach Cognitive Behavioral Therapy (CBT) with a mix of hope and skepticism. It's natural to question whether a series of structured sessions can genuinely unravel the complexities of one's mind. This initial doubt is a common hurdle, often rooted in past disappointments with other treatments or a lack of understanding of CBT. Maintaining motivation and commitment can also be challenging. Life's demands don't pause for therapy; the effort required to engage with CBT exercises can feel overwhelming. It's easy to lose sight of progress, especially when results are brief. These frustrations can sap your resolve, making it tempting to give up.

Take the story of Lisa, for instance. She began CBT with high hopes, only to find herself discouraged when her anxiety persisted. Initial setbacks made her question the effectiveness of the therapy. But Lisa's story didn't end there. With persistence, she found ways to reignite her interest in CBT. Her therapist introduced new techniques tailored to her needs, shifting focus to areas where she felt more in control. This pivot in strategy helped Lisa regain her momentum. She learned to celebrate small victories, like handling a difficult conversation without panic. These achievements, though modest, fueled her commitment to the process. Lisa's perseverance paid off as her anxiety gradually lessened, leading to a richer, more fulfilling life.

Another individual, Tom, faced similar frustrations. He found it difficult to maintain the energy required for consistent CBT practice. The daily grind left little room for introspection, and Tom felt stuck. However, a breakthrough came when he started journaling about his experiences. This simple act of reflection provided clarity and renewed purpose. By writing down his thoughts, Tom could see patterns he hadn't noticed. This insight allowed him to focus on what mattered, rekindling his dedication to CBT. Regularly reviewing his journal entries helped him track his progress, reminding him of the strides he had made. This tangible evidence of growth became a powerful motivator.

The lessons from these experiences are clear: patience and persistence are crucial in therapy. Change doesn't happen overnight, and it's essential to recognize that setbacks are part of the process. Seeking support from therapists or peers can provide encouragement to push through difficult times. Open communication with your therapist is vital. Discussing frustrations or doubts can lead to adjustments in the approach, ensuring that the therapy remains relevant and effective. This dialogue fosters a partnership where the therapist and client work together toward common goals.

For those facing similar challenges, practical strategies can make a difference. Set small, achievable goals to maintain a sense of accomplishment. These milestones can serve as stepping stones, keeping you motivated as you progress. Incorporate techniques that fit naturally into your routine, such as mindfulness exercises during daily activities. This integration reduces the burden of therapy, making it a part of life rather than an additional task. Remember, it's okay to ask for help. External support can offer perspective and encouragement from a therapist, a support group, or loved ones.

As you navigate therapy frustrations, remember that change is a journey marked by ups and downs. Embrace each step, knowing that persistence and adaptability are key. These experiences enrich our understanding, equipping us with the tools to face future challenges with resilience and hope. Transitioning now, we will explore how technology can further support your CBT journey, offering innovative ways to enhance your mental health practice.

8

LEVERAGING TECHNOLOGY IN CBT PRACTICES

I magine standing at a busy intersection, the world buzzing around you, each person on their own path. This scene, with its chaos and rhythm, mirrors the complexity of our thoughts when anxiety and depression weigh heavily. In such moments, reaching out for support can seem daunting, but what if that support was right in your pocket? Technology has revolutionized how we approach mental health, offering tools that empower you to manage your well-being on your terms. One of the most significant advancements is the rise of cognitive behavioral therapy (CBT) apps, designed to provide guidance and support whenever needed. These digital companions are not just apps; they're lifelines that can transform how you engage with your mental health journey.

The variety of CBT apps available today is extensive, each offering unique features tailored to meet different needs. Among the most popular are apps like Woebot and the CBT Thought Record Diary. Woebot, for instance, acts as a digital therapist, engaging users in conversations to help them navigate challenging emotions. It uses artificial intelligence to provide empathetic responses, offering insights that align with CBT principles. The CBT Thought Record Diary, on the other hand, focuses on helping you document and analyze your thoughts. This app encourages you to track moods, identify patterns, and challenge cognitive distortions, supporting the self-reflective practices central to CBT. By providing structured formats for thought logging and guided exercises, these apps empower you to explore your mental landscape with clarity and intention.

The benefits of using CBT apps extend beyond their innovative features. One of the most notable advantages is the accessibility they offer. With these tools, you have on-the-go access to CBT resources, allowing you to engage with therapeutic techniques whenever and wherever you need them. The support is always within reach, whether on a lunch break, commuting, or lying awake at night. This immediacy is particularly beneficial during challenging moments when traditional therapy is unavailable. Having a CBT app at your fingertips means you can access coping strategies and calming exercises in real time, helping you manage anxiety and depression with greater ease.

CBT apps also play a crucial role in facilitating self-guided therapy, empowering you to take charge of your mental health. Many of these apps offer personalized feedback and progress tracking, allowing you to see your growth and identify areas for improvement. This feature can be incredibly motivating, providing tangible evidence of your efforts and achievements. Some apps incorporate gamification elements, such as rewards and milestones, to further engage users. By transforming the therapy process into an interactive experience, these apps make staying committed and proactive in your mental health journey easier.

Consider the experience of a user who struggled with social anxiety. Integrating a _CBT app_ into their daily routine allowed them to practice guided exercises that gradually increased their confidence in social settings. The app provided step-by-step instructions for exposure activities, helping them confront their fears in a structured and supportive manner. Over time, this user reported significant improvements in their ability to engage with others, highlighting the transformative potential of digital CBT tools. Similarly, another individual found relief from mood fluctuations by regularly using a _mood-tracking app_. By documenting their emotions and identifying triggers, they gained a deeper understanding of their mental health patterns, leading to more effective coping strategies and improved overall well-being.

Interactive Element: Exploring Your Ideal CBT App

Take a moment to consider what features would be most helpful for you in a CBT app. Reflect on your unique needs and preferences. Are you seeking mood tracking, guided exercises, or a supportive community forum? Write down your thoughts and explore available apps that align with your criteria. This exercise can help you identify the tools that best support your mental health journey.

Embracing technology in your CBT practice opens up new avenues for growth and healing. Incorporating these digital tools into your routine gives you a flexible and personalized approach to mental health care that complements traditional therapy. The combination of technology and treatment offers a powerful platform for change, empowering you to navigate anxiety and depression with confidence and resilience.

8.1 ONLINE RESOURCES FOR CBT LEARNING

Imagine having a library of CBT knowledge, ready to explore whenever curiosity strikes. The internet has opened doors to an incredible array of resources tailored to help you understand and apply cognitive behavioral therapy in your life. Websites like Psychology Tools and the Centre for Clinical Interventions offer comprehensive educational content on CBT. Psychology Tools, for instance, provides a range of worksheets and guides that delve into various CBT techniques, helping you understand the underlying principles and practical applications. The Centre for Clinical Interventions is another valuable platform known for its evidence-based modules covering anxiety management and mood regulation. These resources are designed to be user-friendly and informative, making them accessible to anyone eager to learn more about CBT.

The beauty of online learning lies in its flexibility. Unlike traditional classroom settings, online resources allow you to learn independently. This self-directed approach means you can revisit concepts as needed, ensuring a more profound understanding of the material. Interactive courses and webinars enhance the learning experience, offering opportunities to actively engage with the content. Webinars provide a dynamic platform where you can listen to experts and participate in discussions, gaining insights from both instructors and fellow learners. This interactive nature enriches your understanding of CBT techniques. It fosters a sense of community, connecting you with others on a similar path.

Choosing the right online resources is crucial to ensure the information you receive is credible and beneficial. Start by checking the credentials of the authors or organizations behind the content. Reliable sources often have affiliations with reputable institutions or are authored by professionals with expertise in CBT. Look for evidence-based resources, meaning they are grounded in scientific research and clinical practice. This credibility ensures that your learning techniques and strategies are effective and safe. Additionally, consider exploring user reviews and feedback to gauge the experiences of others using these resources. This can provide valuable insights into the quality and applicability of the content.

Take Sarah, for example, who wanted to deepen her understanding of CBT to better manage her anxiety. She stumbled upon an online course that blended video lectures and interactive exercises. The course, led by a seasoned therapist, guided her through various CBT techniques, providing real-life examples and practical tips. Sarah found this approach incredibly enlightening, as it allowed her to apply what she learned in her daily life. The flexibility of online learning meant she could fit the course around her busy schedule, revisiting modules whenever she needed a refresher. This self-paced learning empowered Sarah to take control of her mental health journey, equipping her with the tools to navigate her anxiety with confidence.

Similarly, consider Mark, who supplemented his therapy sessions with webinars focused on advanced CBT strategies. These webinars, conducted by experts in the field, offered him a deeper dive into specific techniques like cognitive restructuring and exposure therapy. The interactive format allowed Mark to ask questions and receive personalized feedback, enhancing his understanding and application of these methods. This additional layer of learning reinforced what he was exploring in therapy. It introduced new perspectives and strategies that enriched his overall CBT practice.

The vast wealth of online resources for CBT learning offers a unique opportunity to enhance your mental health toolkit. By exploring credible platforms and engaging with interactive content, you can expand your knowledge and skills, empowering yourself to apply CBT techniques meaningfully. This accessibility and depth of information open new avenues for personal growth and well-being.

8.2 DIGITAL TOOLS FOR TRACKING PROGRESS

In Cognitive Behavioral Therapy, tracking your progress is more than a simple record-keeping exercise. It's a dynamic way to enhance motivation and accountability, offering a mirror to reflect your ongoing journey with mental health. Observing shifts in your mood and behavior over time allows you to identify patterns and improvements that might go unnoticed. This practice turns abstract feelings into concrete data, allowing you to see where you've been and where you might go next. It's like watching your garden grow, each day revealing new buds and blooms that signify change and growth. By consistently monitoring these changes, you create a narrative of progress that can bolster your spirit and reinforce your commitment to personal development.

Numerous digital tools have been developed and designed specifically to track progress in CBT. **Apps like Daylio and Moodpath** are at the forefront, offering intuitive platforms that make mood tracking accessible and engaging. _Daylio,_ for instance, _allows you to log daily moods and activities,_ creating visual progress charts that offer a snapshot of your emotional landscape over weeks or months. These charts can reveal correlations between your activities and mood shifts, offering insights into what supports or hinders your well-being. _Moodpath_ takes this further by providing a _comprehensive mood-tracking experience_ that includes customizable reminders, ensuring you regularly check in with yourself. These features promote consistency in tracking and help you stay connected to your emotional state, fostering a deeper understanding of how your thoughts and behaviors align.

Integrating regular check-ins and review sessions into your routine is essential to maximize the effectiveness of these digital tools. Setting aside time each week to reflect on your data can illuminate trends and trigger points, guiding you in adjusting your CBT strategies and goals. For instance, if your mood consistently dips on Sunday evenings, you might explore ways to create a more relaxing end to your weekend, perhaps by incorporating mindfulness exercises or engaging in a hobby that brings you joy. This process of reflection is not merely about identifying problems but about empowering you to make informed decisions that enhance your mental health.

Consider the story of Lucy, who used a mood-tracking app to help manage her anxiety. By consistently logging her emotions and daily activities, she began to see previously hidden patterns. She noticed that her anxiety peaked during busy workweeks, revealing a need for a better work-life balance. With this insight, Lucy implemented new routines prioritizing self-care, leading to a marked improvement in her well-being. Her story highlights the transformative power of tracking tools, illustrating how they can serve as catalysts for meaningful change. Through this practice, Lucy gained self-awareness and a sense of agency, empowering her to take proactive steps in her mental health journey.

Another narrative comes from Jake, who struggled with self-esteem and depression. Using an app like Moodpath, he diligently tracked his mood fluctuations. He gradually began to understand the factors influencing his emotional state. Over time, Jake discovered that his self-esteem improved when he engaged in physical activity or spent time with loved ones. This realization prompted him to prioritize these activities, leading to a more balanced and fulfilling life. By visualizing his progress through the app's charts, Jake felt motivated to continue his efforts, seeing each step as part of a larger picture of growth.

Reflection Section: Creating Your Tracking Routine

Consider how you might incorporate mood tracking into your daily life. Reflect on what times of day are most conducive to checking in with yourself and how to make this practice a consistent part of your routine. Write down your thoughts and create a simple plan with specific tracking and reflection times. This intentional approach can help you stay accountable and engaged with your progress.

Incorporating digital tracking tools into your CBT practice offers a structured way to engage with your mental health journey. By turning subjective experiences into objective data, these tools provide clarity and direction, helping you navigate the complexities of anxiety and depression with confidence. Whether you're just beginning to explore CBT or looking to deepen your practice, progress tracking can be an invaluable ally, guiding you toward a more resilient and mindful future.

8.3 VIRTUAL THERAPY: WHEN AND HOW TO USE IT

In the digital age, connecting with a therapist has become more convenient. Virtual or online therapy offers a way to receive professional support through platforms like BetterHelp and Talkspace. These platforms provide a space for therapy sessions via video calls, chats, or even phone calls. This approach can be a lifeline for those who find it challenging to attend in-person sessions due to busy sched-ules, physical limitations, or simply the comfort of seeking help from home. Speaking with a therapist from the comfort of your own space can be freeing, removing the barriers that might otherwise prevent you from reaching out.

The benefits of virtual therapy are myriad. Accessibility is perhaps the most obvious advantage; you can connect with a therapist regardless of location if you have an internet connection. This flexibility allows you to fit therapy into your life rather than vice versa. You no longer have to worry about commuting to a therapist's office or taking time off work to schedule an appointment. Furthermore, the comfort of being in your own environment can make it easier to open up, as you're surrounded by familiar sights and sounds. The flexibility of scheduling also means you can find a time that suits you best, whether early in the morning or late at night. This adaptability can make therapy more accessible to those with non-traditional work hours or family responsibilities.

However, like any form of therapy, virtual therapy has its limitations. One potential challenge is the lack of physical presence, making it harder to pick up on nonverbal cues that a therapist might use to gauge your emotional state. While video calls offer visual contact, they can't fully replicate the nuances of in-person communication. Additionally, technical issues such as poor internet connection or software glitches can interrupt sessions, causing frustration and potentially hindering the therapeutic process. It's essential to have a reliable setup to minimize these disruptions. Despite these challenges, many find that the advantages of virtual therapy outweigh the drawbacks, especially when accessibility and convenience are top priorities.

Choosing the right platform and therapist is crucial to ensure quality care when considering virtual therapy. Start by researching the credentials of potential therapists. Look for professionals who are licensed and have experience in treating the specific issues you're facing, whether it's anxiety, depression, or another condition. Platform security is another crucial consideration; ensure your chosen platform complies with privacy standards to protect your personal information. Reading reviews and seeking recommendations can also help you make an informed choice. Taking the time to find a therapist you feel comfortable with can make a significant difference in the effectiveness of the therapy.

Consider the experience of Emma, who found herself frequently traveling for work. The constant movement left her feeling disconnected and unable to maintain regular therapy appointments. Virtual therapy became her solution. With the help of a therapist, she connected with through an online platform, she was able to continue her sessions from hotel rooms and airports, maintaining the continuity of care she needed. For Emma, virtual therapy was a bridge that connected her to the support she needed, regardless of her physical location. Her story highlights the flexibility and accessibility that virtual therapy offers, providing a way to prioritize mental health even amidst a hectic lifestyle.

Another example is Tom, who was initially skeptical about the effectiveness of online therapy. Used to the traditional setting, he wondered if a virtual format could offer the same level of connection and support. However, after a few sessions with a therapist via video call, Tom realized that the ease of accessing therapy from home actually enhanced his willingness to attend regularly. Over time, he found that the therapeutic relationship was just as strong and appreciated the convenience of not traveling. Tom's experience demonstrates how virtual therapy can overcome initial skepticism, offering a viable and effective alternative to in-person treatment.

Virtual therapy opens up new possibilities for accessing mental health care, making it easier for many to seek support. By breaking down geographical and logistical barriers, it provides a lifeline to those who might otherwise struggle to fit therapy into their lives. Whether navigating a busy schedule, living in a remote area, or simply preferring the comfort of your own home, virtual therapy offers a flexible and effective way to engage with professional support. As we continue to explore the intersections of technology and mental health, virtual therapy stands as a testament to the potential of digital solutions to enhance our well-being.

9

LONG-TERM MAINTENANCE AND GROWTH

A s we move through life, it becomes increasingly clear how much we rely on patterns and habits to provide structure and comfort. Picture yourself standing at the edge of a forest, looking at the winding paths before you. Each path represents a different routine you might follow, shaping how you navigate the complexities of daily life. Establishing a routine, particularly in Cognitive Behavioral Therapy (CBT), isn't just about filling your day with tasks. It's about creating a predictable rhythm that calms the mind and reduces anxiety. This predictability acts like a compass, guiding you steadily through life's uncertainties.

Routines are crucial in sustaining CBT practices, mainly as they help reduce anxiety by creating a sense of order. Routines can ground you when life feels chaotic, providing a stable foundation to tackle challenges. They reinforce the effectiveness of CBT techniques by ensuring that these practices become second nature, integrated seamlessly into your life. By committing to a routine, you cultivate a sense of control, which can be empowering in managing anxiety and depression. This control allows you to consistently engage with CBT exercises, enhancing their impact on your mental health.

To create a sustainable CBT routine, schedule dedicated time for your exercises. Whether it's a quiet morning session or a reflective evening practice, setting aside specific times ensures that these moments become a consistent part of your day. Use reminders or cues to prompt practice, like placing a journal by your bedside or setting an alarm for a mindfulness break. These small prompts serve as gentle nudges, encouraging you to regularly engage with your CBT techniques. Over time, these practices will weave into the fabric of your daily life, becoming as natural as brushing your teeth or having your morning coffee.

The benefits of a structured CBT routine extend beyond the immediate practice. Regular engagement with CBT exercises can lead to improved mental health and resilience. As you continue to practice, you'll notice enhanced skill retention and application, with CBT techniques becoming more effective as you grow more familiar with them. This regular practice also increases emotional stability and coping ability, providing a toolkit to easily navigate life's ups and downs. Integrating these practices into your routine creates a foundation for sustained mental well-being, allowing you to face challenges with confidence and resilience.

Consider the story of Anna, who found peace in her morning routine. She starts her day with mindfulness exercises and thought records, setting a positive tone for the hours ahead. This practice allows her to approach each day with clarity and purpose, reducing her anxiety and enhancing her focus. In the evenings, she unwinds with reflection practices that reinforce her

CBT techniques, creating a sense of closure and calm that prepares her for restful sleep. By establishing these routines, Anna has transformed her approach to mental health, finding balance and stability in the predictable rhythm of her day.

Similarly, David has integrated CBT into his evening routine, using the quiet moments before bed to reflect on his thoughts and emotions. He dedicates time to journaling and exploring the day's challenges and victories with an open heart. This practice allows him to process his experiences, fostering a sense of understanding and acceptance. Over time, David has found that these evening reflections reinforce his CBT techniques and provide him with insights that guide his growth and development. By making these practices a regular part of his life, David has cultivated a deep sense of resilience and well-being.

Reflection Section: Creating Your CBT Routine

Reflect on your daily schedule and identify when you can incorporate CBT exercises. Consider your natural rhythms —are you more focused in the morning or evening? Use this awareness to plan your routine. Write down a simple schedule, including specific times and activities. Set reminders to help you stay on track. As you practice, observe any changes in your mental health and resilience. Adjust your routine as needed to ensure it remains supportive and sustainable.

9.1 SETTING REALISTIC GOALS FOR MENTAL HEALTH

Goal setting in the context of Cognitive Behavioral Therapy (CBT) is akin to plotting a course on a map. It provides direction and helps you focus on where you want to go. When dealing with anxiety and depression, goals serve as a roadmap for personal growth and development, giving you a sense of purpose and achievement. Establishing clear goals can boost motivation, as each small success builds momentum for further progress. In CBT, these goals are abstract ideals and concrete, achievable targets that guide your journey toward improved mental health. Setting realistic objectives helps ground you, offering a sense of accomplishment and encouraging you to keep moving forward, even when challenges arise.

Use the _SMART_ criteria to create meaningful and attainable goals: _Specific, Measurable, Achievable, Relevant, and Time-bound_. This framework ensures that your goals are well-defined and realistic, allowing you to monitor progress and stay focused. A specific goal might involve reducing anxiety, but a SMART goal would detail this further: "Attend one social event per week to gradually decrease social anxiety." You can track your achievements and adjust your strategies by making measurable goals. Breaking larger goals into smaller, manageable steps is also crucial. This approach prevents overwhelming feelings and makes it easier to see steady progress. For instance, if your goal is to improve emotional regulation, you might start practicing mindfulness for five minutes a day, gradually increasing the duration as you become more comfortable.

Goal setting plays a crucial role in tracking your progress. These goals are benchmarks for assessing development as you work toward your objectives. Reflecting on your achievements helps you evaluate what has worked and what might need adjustments. This reflection can provide valuable insights into your growth, highlighting areas where you've made strides and others where you might focus more effort. Regularly reviewing your goals keeps you accountable and motivated, reinforcing the positive changes you've made and encouraging further persistence. This process of reflection and adjustment is integral to maintaining momentum and ensuring that your efforts lead to meaningful, lasting change.

Consider the story of Mark, who struggled with social anxiety. He set a goal to attend one social gathering weekly, starting with small, familiar settings. Initially daunting, this goal became more manageable as he gradually exposed himself to different environments. Over time, Mark noticed that his anxiety lessened, and he enjoyed social interactions more. This incremental approach allowed him to build confidence and resilience, transforming a once overwhelming challenge into a source of personal growth.

Similarly, Emily aimed to enhance her emotional regulation through daily mindfulness practice. She started with short sessions, slowly increasing her practice as she became more attuned to her emotions. This consistent effort resulted in greater emotional stability and a more in-depth understanding of her feelings, empowering her to easily navigate life's ups and downs.

Reflection Section: Setting SMART Goals

Take a moment to identify an area of your mental health you'd like to improve. Use the SMART criteria to create a specific, measurable, achievable, relevant, and time-bound goal. Break this goal into smaller steps and write them down. Reflect on how achieving this goal impacts your life and what challenges you face. Consider setting a timeline for reviewing your progress and adjusting your approach as needed. This exercise can serve as a starting point for your journey toward personal growth and development.

9.2 CONTINUOUS GROWTH: ADAPTING CBT OVER TIME

Change is the only constant, and this reality deeply resonates when contemplating the practice of Cognitive Behavioral Therapy (CBT). Your circumstances, challenges, and aspirations will evolve as life unfolds. What worked for you six months ago might not align with your current needs or circumstances. This is why adapting CBT techniques over time is crucial. Consider it a dynamic process that reflects your ongoing growth and changing needs. When you adjust your CBT practices, you ensure they remain relevant and practical, allowing you to tackle new challenges with confidence and resilience. This adaptability is a testament to CBT's strength, offering a tailored approach that evolves as you do.

Adapting CBT practices to meet changing life circumstances involves more than tweaking a few techniques. It's about being attuned to your needs and recognizing when a shift is necessary. This might mean incorporating new exercises or strategies that better fit your current state. For instance, integrating specific stress management techniques could be beneficial if you face new professional challenges. Seeking feedback from therapists or peers can provide fresh insights, helping you refine your approach. They might suggest adjustments you still need to consider, offering a broader perspective on enhancing your CBT practice. This collaborative effort can enrich your journey, ensuring your techniques are practical and aligned with your evolving goals.

The benefits of continuous growth and adaptation in CBT are substantial. By evolving your practices, you prevent stagnation and maintain engagement with your mental health journey. This keeps your approach fresh and relevant, fostering a proactive attitude toward your well-being. When you actively seek ways to improve and adapt, you cultivate a mindset of growth and resilience. This mindset empowers you to face life's challenges with adaptability, knowing you have the tools to navigate whatever comes your way. Continuous adaptation also leads to sustained improvements as you consistently refine your techniques to better serve your needs. This ongoing process of growth ensures that you are always moving forward, building on your strengths, and addressing areas for improvement.

Consider the experience of James, who found himself in a new job that demanded more than his previous role. The pressures of increased responsibility began to weigh on him, affecting his mental health. Recognizing this shift, James adapted his CBT practices to better suit his new professional landscape. He incorporated mindfulness exercises tailored to reduce workplace stress and sought feedback from his therapist to refine his approach. This adaptation allowed James to manage his stress effectively, enabling him to thrive in his role without compromising his mental health. Similarly, Sarah, who had been practicing mindfulness for years, integrated new techniques to deepen her practice. She explored different forms of meditation and incorporated them into her routine, finding that these new practices enriched her existing techniques and provided fresh insights into her mental health.

Interactive Element: Adaptation Checklist

Reflect on your current CBT practices. Identify areas where you could benefit from a change or update. Write down these areas and consider new techniques or exercises that align with your current needs. Seek feedback from a therapist or trusted friend to gain new perspectives. Regularly review and adjust your practices to ensure they remain engaging and effective. This exercise encourages a proactive and flexible approach to your mental health journey.

By embracing the need for adaptation, you allow your CBT practices to grow with you, ensuring they continue to support your mental health and personal development. This adaptability enhances your resilience and empowers you to face life's challenges with confidence and clarity.

9.3 EVALUATING PROGRESS AND MAKING ADJUSTMENTS

Imagine you're traveling on a long road trip, and every so often, you pull over to check your map and ensure you're on the right path. In Cognitive Behavioral Therapy (CBT), pausing to evaluate your progress is equally crucial. Regular assessments give you insight into where you are on your mental health journey, allowing you to make informed decisions about the adjustments needed. By reflecting, you can identify what's working well and what might need a different approach. This ongoing evaluation helps refine your CBT practices, ensuring they align with your evolving needs and goals. It's like tuning an instrument; keeping it harmonious requires attention and care.

Evaluating your progress is more than just a check-in; it's an opportunity to delve into the specifics of your development. Self-assessment questionnaires and reflection logs are one effective way to assess your progress. These tools offer a structured approach to exploring your thoughts, feelings, and behaviors over time. By documenting your experiences, you can spot patterns and changes that may not be immediately apparent. Another valuable resource is seeking feedback from therapists or support groups. They can provide an external perspective, highlighting areas you might overlook. Their insights can be instrumental in helping you understand your progress and identifying potential areas for improvement. This collaborative process enriches your understanding of your mental health, offering a comprehensive view of your development.

Once you've gathered this information, the next step is to make informed adjustments to your CBT practices. This might involve identifying outdated or ineffective techniques that no longer serve you. It's an opportunity to let go of what isn't working and embrace new strategies that address emerging challenges. For instance, if a particular exercise feels stale or unhelpful, consider exploring alternative methods that resonate more deeply with your current state. Incorporating new tools can breathe fresh life into your practice, keeping it relevant and engaging. This process of evaluation and adjustment isn't just about fixing what's broken; it's about evolving your approach to ensure it remains effective and meaningful.

Consider the story of Lisa, who had been using CBT to manage her anxiety. Over time, she noticed that certain techniques were losing their impact. Through regular progress evaluations, she identified these areas and sought feedback from her therapist. Together, they brainstormed new strategies, incorporating mindfulness exercises and creative visualizations that better suited her current needs. This adjustment revitalized Lisa's practices and enhanced her overall engagement with CBT, empowering her to continue growing with renewed energy.

Similarly, Tom found that his initial focus areas in CBT needed a shift as his life circumstances changed. By evaluating his progress and seeking input from his support group, he adjusted his focus, incorporating new tools that addressed previously unmet needs. These changes led to significant improvements in his mental health, demonstrating the power of thoughtful evaluation and adaptation.

Reflection Section: Progress Evaluation

Take a moment to reflect on your current CBT practices. Consider what has been effective and what might need adjustment. Use a reflection log to document your thoughts, identifying patterns and areas for improvement. Seek feedback from a trusted therapist or support group to gain new perspectives. Consider new strategies or tools that enhance your practice. Regularly reviewing and adjusting your approach ensures that your CBT practices align with your needs, supporting your ongoing mental health journey.

9.4 CBT AS A LIFELONG COMPANION

Imagine standing at the start of a winding path that stretches far beyond what you can see yet promises growth and discovery at every turn. Cognitive Behavioral Therapy (CBT) can be likened to a steadfast companion along this path, ever-present as you navigate the complexities of life. Beyond being just a therapeutic method, CBT weaves itself into the fabric of your daily experiences, becoming a part of your mental wellness strategy. It encourages you to view each challenge as an opportunity for growth, helping you build resilience and adaptability. When embraced as a lifelong companion, CBT fosters a mindset that welcomes change and learning, allowing you to confidently face the future.

Maintaining CBT practices throughout life involves more than periodic check-ins; it requires a commitment to integrating its principles into everyday living. Consider CBT not as a temporary fix but as a continuous process of self-improvement and understanding. By doing so, these methods transform into habits that support your mental health even when you're not actively in therapy. Embrace CBT as part of your daily routine, like eating well or staying active. This mindset allows its techniques to become second nature, guiding you in managing thoughts and emotions with clarity and purpose. By cultivating an attitude of continuous learning and adaptation, you remain open to CBT's insights and growth, enriching your life over time.

The benefits of lifelong CBT practice are profound, offering long-term mental health advantages that extend beyond immediate concerns. Sustained engagement in CBT enhances emotional resilience, equipping you with the tools to manage life's inevitable challenges with grace and strength. As you continue to apply these techniques, your capacity for adaptability increases, allowing you to respond to change with greater ease. This adaptability fosters a sense of empowerment as you recognize your ability to influence your mental health positively. Through consistent practice, CBT becomes a source of strength and stability, offering support and guidance, no matter what life throws your way.

Consider the story of Michael, who has integrated CBT into his life for over two decades. Initially introduced to CBT during a particularly challenging period, he found the techniques invaluable in managing his anxiety. Over the years, Michael has maintained these practices, adjusting them as his life evolved. Whether facing career transitions or personal challenges, CBT has been a constant presence, aiding him in navigating each phase with resilience and insight. This long-term relationship with CBT has not only supported his mental health but has also enhanced his personal growth, allowing him to approach new life stages with confidence and curiosity.

Another example is Emma, who began using CBT techniques in her twenties to cope with depression. As she entered different life stages—starting a family and changing careers—Emma found that CBT provided a framework for understanding and adapting to these transitions. The principles of CBT became an integral part of her approach to life, offering guidance and stability amidst change. Emma credits her sustained mental well-being to this lifelong companion, which has helped her cultivate resilience and a complete understanding of herself. By viewing CBT as an ongoing relationship, she has been able to harness its full potential, enriching her life and supporting her mental health through the years.

As you reflect on the role of CBT in your life, consider how its practices can become an enduring part of your mental wellness strategy. By integrating its principles into daily living and embracing it as a lifelong companion, you can unlock its full potential, fostering resilience, adaptability, and personal growth. With CBT, you can face the future confidently, knowing you have a trusted ally in your pursuit of mental well-being. Each chapter of this book builds upon this foundation, inviting you to explore further and deepen your understanding of CBT's transformative power.

10

OVERCOMING BARRIERS AND EMBRACING CHANGE

I remember my grandmother teaching me to ride a bicycle as a child. The initial excitement soon turned into fear as the training wheels came off, and I wobbled across the sidewalk. The fear of falling stopped me from pedaling forward. It wasn't until my grandmother assured me it was okay to be afraid that I found the courage to push past my hesitation. This experience mirrors our resistance when confronted with change, especially involving our mental well-being. Change, while essential for growth, can be daunting. Whether you're trying to break free from negative thought patterns or adopt new coping strategies, resistance often rears its head, whispering that you are not ready. However, understanding why resistance occurs can help you navigate through it.

One of the most common reasons for resistance is the fear of the unknown. Our minds naturally gravitate towards familiar things, even if those familiar patterns contribute to our struggles. The idea of venturing into the unknown, where the outcome is uncertain, can create discomfort. It's much like standing at the edge of a diving board, knowing you have to jump but feeling paralyzed by the fear of what lies below. This natural hesitation makes embracing new routines or behaviors difficult, even when we know they could lead to positive change. Another source of resistance is attachment to habits that, while not beneficial, have become ingrained. These habits provide a sense of security, a known quantity in an unpredictable world. Changing them requires effort and courage; it can feel like letting go of a part of yourself.

The psychological roots of resistance often run deep, intertwined with our beliefs and past experiences. Defense mechanisms like rationalization and denial come into play, providing excuses for why change isn't necessary. You might tell yourself, "It's just the way I am," or "I've tried before, and it didn't work." These thoughts shield us from the vulnerability of attempting change and possibly failing. Past failures and disappointments further contribute to resistance. Each unsuccessful attempt can leave a mark, contributing to a narrative that change is impossible or not worth the effort. Understanding these psychological underpinnings is crucial in dismantling the barriers they create (SOURCE 1).

To overcome resistance, start small. Incremental change is a powerful strategy that involves making minor adjustments rather than overhauling your entire routine at once. For instance, if you're trying to incorporate mindfulness into your day, start with just two minutes of deep breathing each morning. Gradually increase this time as it becomes a natural part of your routine. Visualization exercises can also be effective. Imagine yourself successfully integrating the change and the positive outcomes it brings. Picture the sense of calm, the improved relationships, or the newfound confidence, allowing these images to motivate and guide you.

Alice, a woman I once worked with, perfectly illustrates the power of overcoming resistance. For years, she avoided social gatherings due to anxiety, telling herself she was a homebody by nature. When exploring CBT, she was skeptical and resisted engaging with the techniques. But she started small, committing to attending just one social event per month. She practiced cognitive restructuring with each outing, challenging her negative thoughts about social interactions. Over time, Alice not only attended more events but began to enjoy them, transforming from avoidance to proactive engagement. Her journey shows that change is possible, even when it seems daunting.

Another example is James, who resisted adopting new CBT techniques because past attempts to manage his anxiety had failed. He felt disheartened and skeptical that anything could help. James decided to try again, focusing on incremental change. He started with one technique, journaling his thoughts and emotions each evening. As he became more comfortable with this practice, he integrated other techniques like mindfulness and behavioral activation. Slowly but surely, these practices began to take root, offering him relief and a new perspective on his anxiety (SOURCE 3).

Reflection Section: Overcoming Resistance

Take a moment to reflect on a change you've been resisting. Identify the underlying fears or beliefs that contribute to this resistance. Write them down and explore how they have influenced your behavior. Then, imagine a small step you could take towards embracing this change. Visualize the positive outcomes that could result. Document these thoughts and revisit them when you feel resistance creeping in.

Embracing change is not about eliminating fear but learning to move forward despite it. Understanding the sources of resistance and employing strategies like incremental change and visualization can open the door to new possibilities. These stories and exercises are meant to inspire and guide you, showing that change, while challenging, is within your reach. You build resilience and confidence with each step, transforming resistance into growth.

10.1 ADDRESSING COMMON CBT OBJECTIONS

When you first hear about Cognitive Behavioral Therapy (CBT), it might seem like a complex maze of techniques and theories. Many people wonder if these methods could genuinely apply to their lives. One of the most common objections is that CBT seems too complicated or irrelevant. It's easy to feel overwhelmed by the terminology and the structured approach. You might worry that CBT is too clinical and devoid of the warmth and personal touch that other therapies offer. This perception can make it difficult to engage fully with the process, especially if you're already struggling with anxiety or depression.

Another concern often raised is skepticism about the effectiveness of self-guided therapies. CBT encourages you to take an active role in your healing, which can feel daunting. You might question whether you have the skills or discipline to guide yourself through such a transformative process. Facing your thoughts and emotions without a therapist can be intimidating. Doubts may arise about whether self-guided CBT can genuinely bring about meaningful change or if it is another fleeting attempt at self-improvement. These concerns are valid and common but don't have to be barriers to embracing CBT.

To address these objections, looking at the evidence supporting CBT's efficacy is essential. Research consistently shows that CBT is an effective treatment for various mental health issues, including anxiety and depression. Studies reveal that many individuals experience significant improvement in their symptoms through CBT (SOURCE 4). These findings are not just statistics; they represent people who have found relief and healing through this approach. Additionally, testimonials from individuals who have experienced positive outcomes with CBT can provide reassurance. Hearing stories from others who once shared your skepticism yet found success can be incredibly motivating and inspiring.

Education plays a crucial role in overcoming skepticism about CBT. Understanding the therapy's principles lets you see how it might apply to your life. Participating in informational sessions or workshops can be a great way to learn more about CBT. These sessions often break down the techniques into manageable steps, making them more approachable. They also provide an opportunity to ask questions and address any lingering doubts. The more you understand CBT, the more you can appreciate its potential to foster positive change.

Consider the story of Tom, who was initially doubtful about CBT. He believed the techniques needed to be more flexible and applied to his unique situation. However, after attending a workshop that explained CBT's core concepts and methods, he began to see how they could be tailored to fit his needs. With a newfound understanding, Tom decided to give CBT a try. He started with small, manageable exercises and gradually built up his confidence. Over time, he noticed a shift in his thought patterns and a reduction in his anxiety levels. Tom's experience illustrates how education can transform skepticism into curiosity and willingness to engage with the process.

Peer support can also be a powerful tool in overcoming objections to CBT. Connecting with others on a similar path can provide validation and encouragement. In a support group, you might hear from individuals who have faced similar doubts and how they overcame them. For instance, Lisa found peer support invaluable when hesitating to start CBT. She joined an online community where members shared their CBT experiences. Through their stories, Lisa gained insight into the practical application of CBT techniques and felt less alone in her struggles. This sense of community helped her overcome her reservations and fully embrace the therapy.

CBT may seem intimidating initially, but it becomes more accessible as you learn about its principles and hear from those who have benefited. By addressing common objections and misconceptions, you open the door to a therapy that has the potential to change your life for the better. Embrace the opportunity to explore CBT with an open mind, knowing you are not alone.

10.2 EMBRACING THE PROCESS: PATIENCE AND PERSISTENCE

Experiencing anxiety or depression can feel like standing in front of a mountain, the peak shrouded in clouds, intimidating and seemingly impossible. Cognitive Behavioral Therapy (CBT) requires patience to climb this mountain, as change is not immediate. Instead, it's a gradual process, unfolding slowly, much like the change of seasons. There will be days when the sun shines brightly, progress is visible, and hope is palpable. But there will also be days when clouds gather, and setbacks seem to undo your hard work. Understanding that these fluctuations are natural can help you remain steadfast on your path. Patience is not simply waiting for change but actively engaging with each step, trusting that these efforts will lead you to higher ground.

To cultivate patience and persistence, setting realistic timelines for your goals is crucial. It's easy to get disheartened when results aren't immediate, but true transformation takes time. Break your goals into smaller, achievable milestones. Each small victory is a step closer to the larger goal, like climbing a staircase, one step at a time. Celebrating these little accomplishments can keep motivation alive, fueling your journey. Maybe you managed to counter a negative thought today or attended a social event you would have avoided. These wins matter. They are the building blocks of change, each one reinforcing the foundation of your resilience.

Persistence in CBT is more than just sticking with it; it's about embracing the emotional journey, the highs and the lows. Through consistent practice, you build resilience. Each time you face a challenge and use CBT strategies to navigate it, you strengthen your emotional muscles. This resilience becomes a part of you, a quiet strength that supports you through life's storms. As you persist, you better understand yourself and your growth. You begin to see patterns in your thoughts and behaviors, recognize triggers, and learn how to respond more effectively. This self-awareness is empowering, offering insights that enhance your journey through life.

Consider Sarah, who struggled with depression for years. Initially, she found CBT overwhelming, the exercises and reflections a daunting addition to her already heavy days. But she persisted, setting small, realistic goals. Her first milestone was to get out of bed each morning and write one sentence in her journal. As time passed, those sentences became paragraphs, and soon, she was journaling regularly. As the months passed, Sarah began to notice changes. She felt more in control of her emotions, and her depressive episodes became less frequent. Her story highlights how commitment to the process can lead to profound transformation even when progress seems slow.

Another example is David, who faced severe social anxiety. For him, speaking in groups felt impossible. He started CBT with the simple goal of attending a social event and staying for at least 30 minutes. The first few attempts were challenging, and he often left early, feeling defeated. But he persisted, each time staying a little longer. Gradually, the anxiety began to lessen. He learned to challenge his negative thoughts and embraced small victories, like engaging in a short conversation. After a year of dedicated practice, David found himself not only attending events, but actually enjoying them. His persistence paid off, reshaping his social world.

Patience and persistence in CBT are about more than just enduring. They are about actively participating in your growth and accepting that setbacks are part of the process. Change might not be visible day by day, but over time, the cumulative efforts build a new reality. Each moment of patience, each act of persistence, is an investment in yourself. It's an ongoing dance of effort and reward, where the rhythm of progress is as important as the destination. Through patience and persistence, you will discover that the mountain you once feared is not an obstacle but a landscape of opportunity and growth.

10.3 THE EMPOWERMENT OF SELF-DISCOVERY THROUGH CBT

Cognitive Behavioral Therapy (CBT) is not just a tool for managing symptoms; it is a powerful gateway to self-discovery. This process invites you to look within and understand the intricate dance between your thoughts, emotions, and behaviors. CBT encourages you to explore your inner world with curiosity and compassion. Self-reflection becomes a mirror, showing your strengths and areas ripe for growth. It's about peeling back the layers, not to find flaws, but to reveal the potential that lies beneath. This isn't a path of critique but of understanding, where each insight becomes a steppingstone towards a more authentic version of yourself.

The process of self-discovery through CBT is empowering because it shines a light on the shadowy corners of your mind, illuminating patterns and habits that may have gone unnoticed. As you gain insights into your thoughts and behaviors, you establish a foundation of self-awareness. This awareness is transformative; it offers the clarity needed to make informed choices and enact meaningful changes. With each revelation, confidence grows. You start to see yourself not just as a passive participant in life but as an active agent capable of steering your course. Identifying and understanding these patterns fosters a sense of control and autonomy, moving you from a place of reaction to one of deliberate action.

Engaging in self-discovery requires tools and techniques that allow you to explore your inner landscape. Journaling is one such tool, acting as a conduit for self-reflection. You create a tangible map of your mental and emotional terrain by writing down your thoughts and emotions. This practice encourages you to dig deep, asking questions and seeking answers that reveal the 'why' behind your thoughts and actions. Mindfulness plays a pivotal role. By being present and fully engaged, you cultivate awareness of your immediate experiences, noticing the subtle shifts in thoughts and feelings without judgment. These practices work in tandem to foster a deeper understanding of yourself, unveiling insights that can guide your path forward.

Consider the story of Emma, who discovered hidden talents through CBT. Initially, she struggled with low self-esteem, believing she lacked any special skills. Through journaling and mindfulness exercises, she noticed patterns in what brought her joy. Emma's reflections revealed a passion for storytelling, a skill she had dismissed as trivial. Encouraged by these insights, she decided to explore writing further. As she honed this talent, her confidence blossomed. Emma's journey highlights how self-discovery through CBT can lead to unearthing passions and skills that bring fulfillment and purpose.

Another example is Daniel, who used self-discovery to overcome personal challenges. Daniel battled anxiety, often feeling overwhelmed by life's demands. Through CBT, he learned to identify the thought patterns that triggered his anxiety. Journaling helped him track these patterns, while mindfulness allowed him to stay grounded in the present. Over time, Daniel realized that his anxiety often stemmed from a fear of failure. This pivotal insight enabled him to challenge these fears and adopt healthier coping strategies. Daniel's experience illustrates how self-discovery through CBT can empower you to face personal challenges with newfound clarity and resilience.

By embracing self-discovery, you open up a world of possibilities. Each insight gained is a key that unlocks a door to complete understanding and personal growth. The empowerment from knowing yourself more fully enables you to navigate life's complexities more easily and confidently. It transforms the way you see yourself and your place in the world. As you continue to explore these facets of self-discovery, remember that this process is not about finding definitive answers but embracing the journey of exploration and growth. Through CBT, you cultivate a richer, more nuanced sense of self, ready to engage with the world from a place of strength and authenticity.

CONCLUSION

As you reach the end of this journey through the pages of Cognitive Behavioral Therapy (CBT) for Anxiety and Depression, reflect on the path we've walked together. We've explored the core concepts of CBT, delving into how it can be a powerful ally in managing anxiety and depression. By understanding the foundations of CBT, you've gained insight into how your thoughts influence your emotions and behaviors. We've examined the practical application of CBT techniques, emphasizing the importance of customizing these strategies to suit your individual needs and lifestyle.

Throughout this book, we've highlighted the transformative potential of CBT in changing negative thought patterns and building emotional resilience. You've learned the importance of integrating mindfulness, nutrition, exercise, and spirituality to create a holistic approach to well-being. Each chapter has brought you tools and exercises designed to empower you in your mental health journey. Real-world examples and case studies have illustrated the effectiveness of these strategies, showing that change is possible and within your grasp.

Consider the key takeaways from our discussions. CBT is more than a set of techniques; it's a mindset that fosters growth and resilience. It allows you to alter how you perceive and interact with the world. Integrating holistic practices further supports your mental health, creating a balanced and comprehensive approach to wellness.

Recognize your acquired skills and understanding as you reflect on your journey through this book. You are now equipped with strategies to effectively manage anxiety and depression. Remember that your potential for empowerment and resilience is immense. You can navigate life's challenges with newfound confidence and clarity.

I encourage you to take immediate and ongoing action. Start by applying the CBT techniques and holistic practices in small, manageable steps. As you become comfortable, gradually incorporate more strategies into your daily routine. Let this book serve as a continuous resource for personal growth and mental health management.

Remember, the journey doesn't end here. Maintain a curious and adaptive mindset. Continue learning about CBT and mental health and be open to adapting your strategies as you grow and face new challenges. Seek additional resources, connect with support networks, and engage in lifelong learning to deepen your understanding and skills.

In closing, I want to leave you with a vision of hope and resilience. Managing anxiety and depression is a journey filled with opportunities for growth and empowerment.

Every step you take contributes to your overall well-being and quality of life. Embrace the resilience within you and know that you have the strength to keep moving forward. Pay attention to what you are feeling. Addressing your emotions is the best way to work through it.

Thank you for choosing this book for your mental health journey. Your courage to seek change and improve your well-being is commendable. Remember that you're not alone. With dedication and practice, change is possible. You have the support of this book and the knowledge to guide you on your path. Keep moving forward with hope and resilience, knowing that a brighter future awaits.

If you have found this book helpful, I would appreciate it if you left a favorable review, sharing your reflections and insights so I can continue to help others.

KEEPING THE JOURNEY ALIVE

Now that you have tools and techniques to overcome negative thoughts and build a healthier mindset, it's time to share your insights with others who may be looking for the same support.

By leaving an honest review on Amazon, you're helping others see where they can find the guidance and encouragement they need to start their own journey toward improved mental health.

Thank you for your support. CBT thrives when we share our understanding with others and you're helping me keep this valuable approach accessible to everyone who needs it.

Scan the QR code to leave a review.

— **Dotty Lynn**

REFERENCES

A Brief History of Aaron T. Beck, MD, and Cognitive ... https://www.ncbi.nlm. nih.gov/pmc/articles/PMC9667129/

Cognitive Behavioral Therapy (CBT) vs. Psychoanalysis https://www.grouport therapy.com/blog/cognitive-behavioral-therapy-vs-psychoanalysis

Cognitive Distortions: 22 Examples & Worksheets (& PDF) https://positivepsy chology.com/cognitive-distortions/

Cognitive Behavioral Therapy for Mood Disorders: Efficacy, ... https://www.ncbi. nlm.nih.gov/pmc/articles/PMC2933381/

The Toxic Effects of Negative Self-Talk https://www.verywellmind.com/nega tive-self-talk-and-how-it-affects-us-4161304

Cognitive Reframing: Definition, Techniques, Efficacy https://www.verywell mind.com/reframing-defined-2610419

How to Stop Overthinking: 14 Strategies https://www.healthline.com/health/ how-to-stop-overthinking

Self-Compassion Practices to Deepen Your Resilience https://www.mindful.org/ self-compassion-practices-to-deepen-your-resilience/

CBT in 2023: Current Trends in Cognitive Behavior Therapy https://www. psychiatrictimes.com/view/cbt-in-2023-current-trends-in-cognitive-behavior-therapy

30 Grounding Techniques to Quiet Distressing Thoughts https://www.healthline. com/health/grounding-techniques

CBT for Social Anxiety: How It Works, Examples & ... https://www.choos ingtherapy.com/cbt-for-social-anxiety/

Cognitive Restructuring - Reducing Stress by Changing ... https://www.mind tools.com/aef000n/cognitive-restructuring

Using cognitive behavior therapy to explore resilience in ... https://www.ncbi. nlm.nih.gov/pmc/articles/PMC5047334/

Self-Compassion and Resilience at Work https://self-compassion.org/wp-content/uploads/2021/11/Lefebvre-et-al.-2020-Self-Compassion-and-Resilience-at-Work-A-Practice.pdf

Positive thinking: Stop negative self-talk to reduce stress https://www. mayoclinic.org/healthy-lifestyle/stress-management/in-depth/positive-thinking/art-20043950

Resilience and Mental Toughness: Case Studies and Success ... https://lifecoach
training.co/resilience-and-mental-toughness-case-studies-and-success-
stories/

Mindfulness-Based Cognitive Therapy https://www.psychologytoday.com/us/
therapy-types/mindfulness-based-cognitive-therapy

Nutritional psychiatry: Your brain on food https://www.health.harvard.edu/
blog/nutritional-psychiatry-your-brain-on-food-201511168626

Depression and anxiety: Exercise eases symptoms https://www.mayoclinic.org/
diseases-conditions/depression/in-depth/depression-and-exercise/art-
20046495

Contemporary Perspectives on Spirituality and Mental Health https://www.ncbi.
nlm.nih.gov/pmc/articles/PMC3168074/

CBT Treatment Plan & Example | Free PDF Download https://www.carepatron.
com/templates/cbt-treatment-plans

CBT Techniques: 25 Cognitive Behavioral Therapy ... https://positivepsychol
ogy.com/cbt-cognitive-behavioral-therapy-techniques-worksheets/

Cognitive Distortions: 22 Examples & Worksheets (& PDF) https://positivepsy
chology.com/cognitive-distortions/

4 CBT-Inspired Hacks to Manage Lack of Motivation https://wellnesscounsel
ingserviceslcsw.com/4-cbt-inspired-hacks-to-manage-lack-of-motiva
tion/

Social anxiety: How cognitive behavioral therapy can help https://www.cnn.
com/2022/04/01/health/social-anxiety-cognitive-behavioral-therapy-
benefits-wellness/index.html

Using CBT in the Treatment of Depression https://theprivatetherapyclinic.co.
uk/blog/treatment-of-depression/

Religiously Integrated Cognitive Behavioral Therapy https://www.ncbi.nlm.nih.
gov/pmc/articles/PMC4457450/

Overcoming Obstacles in CBT https://uk.sagepub.com/en-gb/eur/overcom
ing-obstacles-in-cbt/book234702

MindShift® CBT App https://www.anxietycanada.com/resources/mindshift-
cbt/

Best Online Cognitive Behavioral Therapy (CBT) in 2024 https://www.everyday
health.com/emotional-health/best-online-cognitive-behavioral-ther
apy/

Mood Tracker: How to Use, Types, Benefits https://www.verywellmind.com/
what-is-a-mood-tracker-5119337

Virtual Therapy Vs. In-Person Therapy https://www.psychology.org/
resources/virtual-therapy-vs-in-person/

CBT Techniques: 25 Cognitive Behavioral Therapy ... https://positivepsychol
ogy.com/cbt-cognitive-behavioral-therapy-techniques-worksheets/

SMART Goals \u0026 Mental Health https://www.mhddcenter.org/wp-
content/uploads/2021/01/SMART-Goals-Mental-Health.pdf

Adapting Cognitive Behavioral Therapy to Each Client https://www.psychology
today.com/us/blog/all-about-cognitive-and-behavior-therapy/202110/
adapting-cognitive-behavioral-therapy-each

Long-term Outcomes of Cognitive Behavioral Therapy for ... https://www.ncbi.
nlm.nih.gov/pmc/articles/PMC6902232/

The Psychology of Resistance to Change https://www.ncbi.nlm.nih.gov/pmc/
articles/PMC8365138/

Is it possible to convince a skeptic that therapy can work? https://www.quora.
com/Is-it-possible-to-convince-a-skeptic-that-therapy-can-work

Strategies for Incorporating CBT Techniques into Daily Life https://cpdonline.
co.uk/knowledge-base/mental-health/cbt-techniques-daily-life-strate
gies/

Empowerment through CBT Therapy: Tools for Personal ... https://holland-
pearse.com/empowerment-through-cbt-therapy-tools-for-personal-
growth/

Printed in Great Britain
by Amazon

62798737R00092